RATIONING IN ACTION

RATIONING IN ACTION

Published by the BMJ Publishing Group
Tavistock Square, London WC1H 9JR

First Published 1993

Second Impression 1994

British Library Cataloguing in Publication Data
A catalogue record for this book is available from the British Library

The following picture sources are acknowledged:
page 36, Oregon Legislative Media Services; page 62, Margaret Cooter; page 99, Mary Evans Picture Library.

Typeset, printed and bound in Great Britain by
Latimer Trend & Company Ltd, Plymouth

Contents

Introduction

The debate on rationing, or priority setting, in health care has finally begun in earnest, and this book is a contribution to that debate. It is much nearer to being the first rather than the last word, but it does include data and accounts of real experience as well as fine words. People who have never thought about the issue will find the book accessible, and those who have studied the subject will also find much that is useful.

The book has grown out of a conference organised jointly by the BMJ, the BMA, the King's Fund, and the Patients Association and held in March 1993. The conference had the aim of bringing the debate on rationing to a wider audience. The central conviction, from which few people dissent, is that this is far too important a subject to be left to one group. There is some sense in the book, and in the broader debate, of politicians, doctors, managers, and others trying to pass the buck to each other, but most contributors accept that everybody has a contribution to make to the debate and to the painful decisions that must be taken.

The book begins, as did the conference, with a discussion on whether rationing is inevitable. Doctors know that they do not have the resources to do everything possible for all of their patients—and they never have had: for a start, and very obviously, their own time has to be rationed. Politicians know that not everything can be a priority but tend to feel queasy about the word rationing. (Some controversy surrounded the word rationing in the conference title being changed to priority setting in order to make sure that the secretary of state for health would speak.) For economists the central question of their whole subject is how to distribute finite resources, and managers every day have to make hard choices on where to allocate resources.

Most groups—except perhaps patients—thus understand well that rationing is inevitable, but there was some reluctance to accept this at the conference because of the fear that the government would be let off the hook of providing adequate resources for the health service. This is a real worry for health professionals: can they play a responsible part in this important debate without seeming to condone what many of them see as underfunding of the health service?

After the first two chapters come the thoughts of the secretary of state for health, Virginia Bottomley. She insists that clinical priorities must be set locally, not nationally, and rejects as "flawed" the Oregon approach that is described in the following chapter by John Kitzhaber, a doctor and former president of the Oregon senate, who was central in the development of the approach. Mrs Bottomley says that "understanding the effectiveness of clinical interventions is the key to proper priority setting," and most doctors would agree that establishing good evidence on effectiveness—and on costs—is crucial.

But many would still argue—as does Dr Kitzhaber—that no health system will be stable unless is answers the question of what is covered. No health system has yet answered that question adequately and no health system is stable: the two may well be cause and effect. Dr Kitzhaber describes how the Oregonians have tried to answer the question and Dr R L J M Scheerder from the Netherlands describes how the Dutch have attempted an answer. Nobody has found it easy, but the Oregonians and Dutch are well ahead of the British. Chris Ham from Birmingham describes the first faltering steps in six British health districts.

Part III of the book looks at how the disciplines of sociology, philosophy, and economics can contribute to the debate on rationing. In essence, they have well tested techniques to offer. Rudolf Klein from Bath argues that decisions on allocating resources are taken at a multiplicity of levels within the NHS and that to make priority setting more rational we must concentrate on the processes and structures of decisions making; the debate must be rational, informed, and open and involve a plurality of interests. "Our aim," he concludes, "must be to build up, over time, our capacity to engage in continuous, collective argument."

The sections that follow look at what rationing means to various participants in health care. Chris Heginbotham presents the results of surveys conducted specifically for the conference;

this was the first time that the same questions had been put simultaneously to patients, doctors, and managers. The results show widely divergent thinking, and clearly the debate must be taken into a still broader public arena. Toby Harris from the Association of Community Health Councils considers how the public can be brought more into the debate.

Since the conference, various television and radio programmes have covered the subject, and public debate has been inflamed by cases of surgeons denying coronary artery bypass operations to smokers, by a single mother giving birth to sextuplets after treatment for infertility, and by postmenopausal women being offered in vitro fertilisation. Inevitably, the public debate that has surrounded these issues has been confused and moralistic at times, but the cases do provide an impetus for debate that more theoretical discussions rarely manage to equal.

In the final section of the book we publish several editorials, papers, and letters on rationing that have appeared in the BMJ in the past two years. We hope that these pieces and the whole book will contribute to the "continuous, collective argument" identified by Rudolf Klein.

RICHARD SMITH
Editor, *BMJ*
July 1993

PART I:
THE DEBATE

1 Is rationing inevitable?

TREVOR A SHELDON, ALAN MAYNARD

The debate about rationing is characterised by confusion and sharp practices as vested interests, both professional and commercial, manipulate policy makers and the community. Rationing is inevitable. The real issue is how it should take place to ensure that health care is provided equitably and efficiently.

Scarcity

It is the ubiquitous nature of scarcity that makes rationing inevitable. Because the demands of individuals, groups, and society exceed the available resources to fund the acquisition of goods and services, choices have to be made—resources must be allocated or rationed between competing ends.

The consequence of scarcity in health care is that there are always health care activities that people need but that are not available. In Britain, harsh choices are made which deprive people—sometimes on waiting lists, sometimes undiagnosed in the community—of care from which they may benefit. In the United States, which spends twice as much on health care per capita as does Britain, social choices deprive 35 million people of health insurance.

In all spheres of activity rationing, or choices about who will get access to what services at what cost, is inevitable. Such choices in health care tend to be particularly emotional as no one likes to see fellow humans in distress that could be mitigated by medical interventions. However, rationing takes place at each level of all health care systems.

In Britain each year there is competition for scarce public expenditure, and the Department of Health bids to the Treasury for additional resources. The product of Cabinet horse trading is an allocation of resources for health care to the constituent parts of the United Kingdom, typically characterised by "generous" resourcing to Scotland and Ulster.[12] Each of these budgets is then rationed among the purchasers in each country.

In England the Department of Health "top slices" resources to fund itself and the NHS Management Executive, currently consuming £0.3bn, and allocates the rest by a weighted capitation formula to the 14 regions. The regions top slice their allocations—that is, they make choices to fund their own activities and regional specialties—before allocating the remainder, usually also by such formulas, to purchasers, family health services authorities, and general practitioner fundholders. These purchasers then make choices about how to spend their limited budgets by buying the services of providers—for instance hospitals, pharmaceuticals, and staff.

At each level of this resource allocation system choices are made and scarce resources are allocated to competing suppliers of services. These rationing processes reward some and penalise others—that is, some providers win access to funding and the capacity to provide care and others fail. Those who fail will use personal advocacy, rhetoric, and shroud waving in the media to highlight the deficits in funding and the "errors" of the purchasers. They will assert that if funded they could provide care which might benefit (improve the health) of their patients. However, rationing is unavoidable: some patients will inevitably be deprived of care from which their clinicians believe they could benefit. This is the nature of the rationing system in the NHS: who will live, in what degree of pain and discomfort, when all must ultimately die?

As the competition for resources becomes more intense and better defined the mystique of the medical profession will be challenged increasingly. Doctors will be treated like non-clinical managers who have no mystique (and therefore less public legitimacy) with which to protect their rationing decisions. Managers and clinicians will be drawn together to confront that fundamental element in everyone's life: the need to ration. As Mechanic argued:

4

"As people have learned to have high and more unrealistic expectations of medicine, demands for care for a variety of conditions, both major and minor, have accelerated. No nation that follows a sane public policy would facilitate the fulfilment of all perceptions of need that a demanding public might be willing to make. As in every other area of life, resources must be rationed."[3]

Methods of rationing

How can scarce resources be rationed between competing demands? In most markets the price mechanism is used. Those willing and able to pay get access to apples, cars, computer games, and medical journals. Those willing and able to pay health insurance premiums can get access to health care differentially from those with only NHS "rights" to care.

There are many other ways in which access to health care can be rationed. Some of these are listed in the box and are not mutually exclusive. Many of these rationing mechanisms are deployed in various, largely unchartered ways in the NHS; that is, the rationing process is implicit, and those who ration do not have their choices monitored and evaluated and are largely not accountable for the ways in which funds are deployed.

The founding fathers and mothers of the NHS stated in the 1946 NHS Bill that it "imposes no limits on availability, e.g. limitation based on financial means, age, sex, employment or vocation, area of residence or insurance qualification."[5] This was a nice statement of how resources were not to be rationed. However, politicians then and subsequently have been less clear about how scarce NHS resources should be allocated. In keeping with socialist principles Margaret Thatcher argued in her 1982 speech to the Conservative party conference that "the principle that adequate health care should be provided for all, regardless of their ability to pay, must be the foundation of any arrangements for financing health care."

Thatcher and her predecessors, Conservative and Labour, did not (openly) wish to allocate resources by willingness and ability to pay. However, their definition of the alternative rationing criterion, "need," was less than precise. Williams explored competing definitions of need: is it a supplier's criterion of effectiveness or a demander's notion of ability to benefit?[6] The concept of need as ability to benefit is appropriate as the principle guiding access to health care for those who reject the market and prefer more collective mechanisms in health care markets.[7]

The implication of this is that one principle which should guide resource allocation in the NHS is the patient's capacity to benefit per unit of cost. Resources should be targeted at those patients for whom medical intervention is cost effective. Those for whom the costs of treatment are high and the benefits (in terms of enhancement in the length and quality of life) are low will be accorded less priority and may be denied treatment. This may result in discrim-

Forms of rationing: a continuum of government involvement

Form	*Criteria used*	*Effects on health care*
Physician's discretion	Medical benefit to patient Medical risk to patient Social class or mental capacity	Reinforces technological imperative Increases costs with no constraint on major access points Reinforces differential access
Competitive marketplace	Ability to pay	Creates tiered access system Leads to elaborate charity system
Insurance marketplace	Ability to pay for insurance Group membership Employment	Encourages use of resources Escalates demand and costs of health care Spreads risk and thus expands access
Socialised insurance (Medicaid)	Entitlement	Covers people lacking adequate private insurance Increases role of government in medical decision making Increases cost to public Creates new tiered system of public *v* private sector patients

Implicit rationing ↓	The queue Limited staffing and facilities Medical benefits to patient with consideration of social costs	Imposes shortage of some health care Increases role of government in regulation and budgeting Limits access to specialists Reinforces tiered system Shifts emphasis toward social benefits and costs
Explicit rationing ↓	Triage Medical benefit to patient with emphasis on social costs and benefits Strict allocation	Limits high cost care with dubious benefits Makes peer review mandatory Imposes cost containment measures Imposes regulation of private as well as public sector Bureaucratises rationing
Controlled rationing	Equity in access to primary care Social benefit over specific patient benefits Cost to society	Eliminates private health care sector Fully bureaucratises medical decision making Limits discretion of patient, physician, and other health providers Imposes strict regulation and control of all facets of medicine Eliminates tiered system

Source: Blank[4], Figure 3.1.

ination or rationing resources away from groups such as the elderly. However, this may not always be the case—for example, there is evidence of rationing in coronary care units and of thrombolytics, which disadvantages elderly patients,[8] even though such treatments may be cost effective.[9]

Consequently it is important to determine resource allocation by cost effectiveness data on identified subgroups of patients rather than by global rules to discriminate against groups such as the elderly (as advocated by Callaghan[10 11]). Although this is a general

7

principle of rationing, the technology for making these "rational" choices is, as yet, poorly developed and cannot be isolated from the politics of choice.

Resource allocation in the NHS

The consequence of allocating or rationing resources by ability to benefit is that the purpose of the NHS is to improve health. Often this is not evident from the policy debate, which focuses on the sectional interests of professions anxious to enhance empires and politicians determined to retain power.

How much should a nation spend on health care?

The response of providers to this question is, more. However, caution is essential: the United States spent more than $830 billion on health care in 1992 (over 14% of gross domestic product), yet many people do not have access to efficient health care. The Princeton economist Uwe Reinhardt mocked the United States's situation, extrapolating the inflation of recent expenditure to the year 2100 and finding that 81.5% of gross domestic product would be spent on health care (personal communication, below).

An American health spending scenario

Omniscient Expert: During the 1980s, the average annual growth of health spending outgalloped the rest of gross domestic product (GDP) by about 3 percentage points. During the preceding period, 1965–80, that growth differential was pretty much the same. American health policy works; therefore view that differential as an American tradition—as a natural constant, so to speak, like e or pi. Alas, the Congressional Budget Office now predicts that, during the 1990s, the differential will widen to about 4.7 percentage points, mainly because GDP is limping along so slowly. The office projects that, by the year 2000, fully 18% of the GDP will go to health care.

Incredulous Lay Person: Good heavens! Soon we'll spend 100% of the GDP on health care!

Omniscient Expert: Relax! That can't happen. Even at a differential of 4.7 percentage points, only about 96% of the GDP would go to health care in the year 2100. But let's not be alarmist. Suppose that, after the year 2000, the growth differential dropped once again to the more staid, traditional 3 percentage points. Then only about 50% of the GDP would go to health care by the year 2050, leaving fully half of the GDP for the other good things in life. And even by the year 2100, only 81.5% of the GDP would go to health care; there would still be some room for other things.

Incredulous Lay Person: Health care eating over 80% of the GDP by the year 2100?! Is such a thing even conceivable?

Omniscient Expert: In principle, yes. American would be covered from coast to coast with king sized beds, made by Mercedes Benz. Each bed, fully loaded with a myriad of imaging devices made by Sony, would be occupied by two Americans, each equipped with an MD degree and with multiple artificial body parts made by Aero Spatiale, Mitsubishi, Rolls Royce, and Siemens. Through giant transoceanic pipelines these fully medicalised Americans would be fed intravenously with scrumptious nutrients prepared by the finest chefs in France and China. The MDs would give each other hourly check ups, continuous body scans, and ever more stunning transplants. The bills they would send to one another would add up to 81.5% of the GDP. Voila!

Incredulous Lay Person: And who would produce the rest of the GDP?

Omiscient Expert: It would be produced by non-medicalised, uninsured, low wage American workers and their families who, of course, would not be entitled to a bed. These workers would assemble some of the body parts Stateside under foreign licence because, to be classified as an "American" in the year 2100, at least 20% of a person's body parts will have to have been "manufactured" in the USA.

Incredulous Lay Person: Could America at that time actually pay for the imported beds, body parts, and scrumptious intravenous fluids?

Omniscient Expert: In principle, yes. America financed its joyous consumption boom during the 1980s partly by running huge trade deficits, which were paid off in part by surrendering to foreigners most of Hawaii, huge chunks of California, and most of Fifth Avenue in New York, along with numerous American corporations. But, wisely, America kept a good many companies in reserve, along with Arkansas, Nebraska, and many other fine states. This vast reserve could be used to finance future trade deficits. In a pinch, the foreign suppliers might even take New Jersey and General Motors.

Incredulous Lay Person: But would any of these be dumb enough literally to give itself away for health care?

Omniscient Expert: In principle, no. No nation would be that silly. In

9

practice, yes, because to do otherwise might force Americans to *ration* health care. The uninsured aside, *rationing* health care is just not an American thing. Canadians and Europeans do that, which is precisely what makes these aliens so un-American.

The need to ration, which the Americans are just beginning to debate (although it has always been there), makes it essential that the cost effectiveness of interventions competing for funding is identified. Typically, investments in all activities, including health care, exhibit diminishing returns in terms of health benefits, and all involve opportunity costs (that is, alternative investments have to be forgone). In decisions on how much to invest in health care, the value of the benefits and opportunity costs has to be compared with the value produced by investments in housing, education, roads, water, and sewerage. Such values will inform social choices and rationing decisions between competing sectors.

At present these choices are poorly informed. The marginal benefits and costs of health care practices are unknown, and as a consequence it is impossible to determine whether the "right amount" is being spent on health care. The development of "medical Disneylands" may have more to do with the lifestyles of providers than the efficient production of health for the population. It is likely that health would be more beneficially influenced by expenditure in the social and environmental spheres than by much of the current expenditure in the NHS.

Rationing in the health service

The primary agents in the rationing of services delivered to patients are the clinicians, who feel that it is their experience which makes them best fit to decide who will get access to care. It is the priorities of the clinicians that have driven the health care system, usually with no regard to cost. The risk that choices will be predicated by self interest—power—rather than patient interest is considerable because of the mystique of the profession and pervasive ignorance about cost effectiveness.

This ignorance has been recognised for many years. A debate about hospital efficiency in the early 1840s led the editor of the *Lancet* to advocate the measurement of hospital outcomes: "All public institutions must be compelled to keep case-books and registers, on a uniform plan. Annual abstracts of the results must be published. The annual medical report of cases must embrace hospitals, lying-in hospitals, dispensaries, lunatic asylums and prisons."[12] This advocacy affected legislation, and the Lunacy Act required hospital managers and clinicians in psychiatric hospitals to measure their success in terms of whether patients were dead, relieved, or unrelieved. These data were collected throughout the nineteenth century and the classification was advocated by Florence Nightingale for the acute sector.[13] These concepts are ambiguous (how do you measure relief?) but they are sophisticated compared with routine NHS information systems, which often cannot distinguish between vertical and horizontal discharges.

All health care systems today are characterised by wide variations in clinical practice, few data about the effectiveness of interventions, even fewer data about outcomes and the cost effectiveness of care and cure, and considerable ignorance about how to change clinical behaviour even when it is possible to guestimate and target efficient practice. The policy makers' response to an often incomplete and poor definition of these problems is to limit public expenditure, but such pressure alone is insufficient. New technologies should be evaluated to determine their cost effectiveness before they are disseminated widely. Such evaluation involves the measurement of clinical outcomes, health outcomes, and costs. The resultant knowledge can be used to determine whether purchasers will reimburse new methods of care. This approach has been adopted by Australia, which now requires pharmaceutical companies to provide cost effectiveness data when applying for the reimbursement of their new drugs from Medicare.

The techniques of cost effectiveness analysis can be complemented by consumer surveys, consensus conferences, meta-analyses, and a variety of other mechanisms.[14] The purpose of these techniques is to focus decision makers' attention on the relevant information (cost effectiveness) to inform rationing to encourage practitioners and suppliers to identify, measure, and value the costs and effects of competing treatments. Such activity will facilitate the creation of guidelines for clinical practice. These are essential for effective clinical audit and the establishing of proper accountability.

Who should prioritise? The contribution of the expertise of clinicians and other professionals into the rationing process is important but is only one element in determining society's preferences. This perspective must be complemented by careful consideration of outcomes and costs carried out at the national level. At present the British government seems to favour delegating all the apparatus of rationing to the local level. This will inevitably lead to duplication, confusion, and inefficiency. At least the technical information on which rationing should be based needs to be coordinated nationally; standards must be agreed nationally and evaluative resources carefully targeted to ensure their efficient use.

That rationing is inevitable is not worth more debate; that rationing is a powerful mechanism to promote an efficient and equitable service has not been so obvious. What is less easy is to determine how to translate progressive aims of rationing into practice. The technologies of rationing from various disciplinary perspectives that have been put forward include cost-QALY league tables, voting, surveys, and consensus conferences. There is no single approach to developing a "correct" set of rationing criteria and decisions.

Whatever technology is used, local rationing decisions must become part of the political process and have the democratic participation of local people. This is not currently possible owing to the lack of democratic accountability of health authorities. As long as there is no public accountability, rationing will continue to look like government subterfuge to cut resources and indeed is more likely to become so.[15] However, if democratic decisions are not properly informed by the scientific evidence, the discussion of rationing will be confused both by the disingenuous arguments of some of the political left, who argue that rationing can be avoided solely by more funding and by the self interest of profit making corporations and cosy professional cabals and the vigour of occasional enthusiasts. Such confusion will produce unethical medical practices. If health care resources are not allocated to those who can benefit most (per unit of cost) there is inefficiency. Inefficiency deprives potential patients of care from which they would benefit and is unethical. Waiting lists may be efficient and ethical. Only if patients on such lists would derive more benefit by being seen now rather than later are they inefficient devices to ration care.[16]

Rationing is unavoidable, and if we want a service that uses the public's money to promote health in an efficient and equitable way we should not just sit back and accept it as a necessary evil. Instead, it is important to get involved in rationing to ensure that it occurs in a responsible and just fashion rather than the current process, which is largely unchartered and the product of clinical discretion which creates major variations in practice and patient access. Without the evaluation of practices, the establishment of clinical guidelines, and the effective audit of behaviour, resources are unlikely to be used efficiently.

Rationing on the basis of scientific knowledge is efficient, ethical, and inevitable. It will be demanded by a society whose members increasingly perceive the deficiencies in medical practice and the need to challenge the medical mystique.

Conclusions

Rationing has always existed in the NHS but there has been a tendency to ignore it (except, for instance, in areas such as transplantation, where criteria are long established) and to rediscover it regularly in the "crisis" phase of the NHS funding cycle. The existence of rationing should be accepted, and the focus of policy debate and research activity should be how to implement more efficient and equitable rationing processes in the face of ignorance both about what works in health care and how inefficient behaviours can be changed. Such processes will produce political and clinical challenges because they will increase public accountability. However, some science and more openness are to be preferred to the present practices, which are fake—that is, characterised by contriving out of poor material. Ignorance and poor science are barriers to efficient and equitable rationing processes in health care and are intolerable.

1 Maynard A, Ludbrook A. Applying the resouce allocation formulae to the constitutent parts of the UK. *Lancet* 1980; **i**: 85–7.
2 Birch S, Maynard A. *The RAWP review: RAWPing the United Kingdom.* York: Centre for Health Economics, University of York, 1986. (Discussion paper 1a.)
3 Mechanic D. The growth of medical technology and bureaucracy: implications for medical care. *Milbank Memorial Fund Quarterly* 1977; **55**: 61–78.
4 Blank RH. Rationing medicine. New York: Columbia University Press, 1988.
5 Ministry of Health. *The National Health Service Bill: a summary of the proposed service.* London: HMSO, 1946. (Cmnd 6761.)
6 Williams A. Need as a demand concept. In A J Culyer, ed. *Economic policies and social goals.* London: Martin Robertson, 1974: 60–76.
7 Maynard A, Williams A. Privatisation and the National Health Service. In: Le Grand J, Robinson R, eds. *Privatisation and the welfare state.* London: Allen and Unwin, 1985: 95–110.
8 Dudley NJ, Burns E. The influence of age on policies for admission and thrombolysis in coronary care units in the United Kingdom. *Age and Ageing* 1992; **21**: 95–8.
9 Krumholtz HM, Pasternak RC, Weinstein MC, Friesinger GC, Ridker PM, Tosteson ANA, *et al.* Cost effectiveness of thrombolytic therapy with streptokinase in elderly patients with suspected acute myocardial infarction. *N Engl J Med* 1992; **327**: 1, 7–13.
10 Callahan D. *Setting limits: medical goals in an ageing society.* New York: Simon and Schuster, 1987.

11 Callahan D. *What kind of life: the limits of medical progress*. New York: Simon and Schuster, 1990.
12 [Editorial.] Lancet 1840–1; i: 649–53.
13 Nightingale F. *Some notes on hospitals*. 3rd ed. London: Longman, 1863.
14 Drummond MF, Maynard A, eds. *Purchasing and providing cost-effective health care*. Edinburgh: Churchill Livingston, 1993.
15 Pollock AM. Rationing—implicit or merely complicit? *Critical Public Health* 1993; 4: 19–23.
16 Williams A. Priority setting in a needs based system. In: Gelijus AC, ed. *Technology and health care in an era of limits*. Washington, DC: National Academy Press, 1993: 79–95.

2 Getting a quart out of a pint pot

CHRISTINE HANCOCK

Demand for health care seems to increase daily. Health care professionals, politicians, journalists, and commentators regularly state that demand for health care is infinite and that because resources are finite, this demand simply can't be met in full.

Today health services throughout the world focus on rationing as the major dilemma facing them in the 1990s. In the United Kingdom, with its new internal market of purchasers and providers, rationing and priority setting are heralded as central issues for purchasers as they seek to reconcile the economic reality of limited resources with which to meet increasing demand and public expectations.

Perhaps inevitably, people are not asking whether rationing is necessary, but rather how it can be done. Evidence suggests that rationing already takes place covertly and that it always has done. So the need for rationing is accepted and health authorities are called upon to be "honest" and to explore explicit rationing, usually involving some kind of open, public debate—or at any rate, removing rationing decisions solely from the hands of the medical and health care professionals. But is it true to say that demand for health care is infinite? Or even that the resources available to meet that demand are finite?

This chapter questions the common assumption of limited resources and unlimited demand, questioning the validity of a system of explicit rationing in today's health care system but emphasising the usefulness of exploring public health values.

As new drugs and surgical techniques are developed and more people live considerably longer, so invariably the demand for health care increases. We will always have to deal with accidents and emergencies, and in this age of large scale industrial catastrophe we can expect no let up there.

But ultimately, is demand for health care infinite? After all, many diseases have been eradicated completely, at least in the Western world, and we all have a finite number of limbs and organs to be replaced, removed, or remodelled. Are we really sitting on a complex mass of health problems just waiting to explode as soon as we know they can be treated? And just because medical science is increasingly capable of prolonging life, will patients necessarily welcome more medical intervention and perhaps more discomfort at the expense of greater quality of life?

We already possess and can often predict with a high degree of accuracy the incidence of disease in a lifetime, the cost and nature of the treatment, the requirements for preventing the disease, and how much of a threat it is to life. We can predict the number of births and deaths year to year, and we can estimate the health needs of the community in terms of, say, how many hip replacements or how many long stay psychiatric beds will be required. Are we sure that demand could not be met completely with a relatively modest increase in resources?

If demand were to be met in full, and care was available—unrationed and as soon as it was needed—we could avoid costly and unnecessary problems associated with waiting for treatment, ranging from depression and stress to immobility and total dependence. This does not include the enormous cost to business of lost production, or the cost of sickness and other social benefits.

In reality, many groups have an interest in the costs and benefits of speedy and effective treatment, and there is a strong case for investing in research to establish the extent of potential cost savings. Certain government departments might find it cost effective to transfer part of their budgets to the health service to ensure early and effective treatment. In a private company, internal departments budget in this way. So while we in the United Kingdom have created an internal market for health care, perhaps we are not market orientated enough.

A bottomless pit?

If we assume for a moment that the pit is not bottomless—that it could be possible to treat everyone who needed treatment—the question is, how close to the bottom of the pit are we?

On the surface it seems that resources for health care are severely limited. But it is not necessarily the case that the resources allocated to health care should remain at their present, inadequate level. Perhaps some of the money and effort presently spent on exploring new and equitable ways of allocating "scarce" resources could be used to put the case for increasing current expenditure or on actually providing some of those essential services.

But the resources available to us to meet increasing, if not infinite, demand may not necessarily be finite. Even outside the sphere of our health services there are infinite resources available to meet much of the demand.

I accept that fast and effective clinical services will always be necessary, and indeed improving them could well prove to be cost effective over the longer term, but activating some of the unlimited resources at our disposal requires more of a focus on health gain for communities. In spite of all the attention being paid to prevention and health promotion—to primary health care—our health services remain sickness services with most resources devoted to last minute repairing of problems that could have been prevented or treated earlier.

Key performance indicators of success in most countries are increases in the numbers of people who are being treated in hospitals, even though hospital treatments are marginal to the health of the population. Many research studies and practical experiments show what can be achieved in many areas: reducing hospital length of stay,[1] lowering prescribing costs, lessening the rates of iatrogenic diseases and complications.[2] Yet too often such studies have not been widely put into practice and experiments remain just that.

Meanwhile health care is still very much defined as medical care. For nurses, this definition denies the contribution that they and others make to patient's wellbeing. Yet nursing does have a valuable and unique contribution to make to people's health. A growing number of research studies show categorically that nursing has a positive effect on patient outcomes, and in many

17

> ### An infinite resource
> - Nursing is often more effective than drugs—and at half the price
> - Over the past decade the number of nurses working in general practice has increased by 1200%
> - With appropriate support staff, the size of general practitioners' lists could be doubled, or services on offer could be expanded
> - Nurses' role as educators and facilitators places an infinite resource at the disposal of their clients

situations it is often more effective than drugs.[3] And of course at half the price.

Nurses as a resource

Nurses are currently very concerned with the issue of skill mix in health care, and the Royal College of Nursing is committed to demonstrating the cost effectiveness of employing higher ratios of qualified nurses to less qualified staff. But some research commissioned by the college and carried out at the Centre for Health Economics at the University of York points out the cost savings from employing qualified nurses in general practice compared with general practitioners.[4]

By the college's own arguments, it would of course be necessary to analyse the cost effectiveness of any changes in the skill mix in general practice by looking at its impact on the quality of care provided. But from our perspective of health promotion and achieving maximum health gain in the community, the figures make interesting if not comfortable reading.

General practitioners have increasingly employed nursing staff in the past two years. In fact, over the past 10 years the number of practice nurses has increased by 1200%. This has allowed general practitioners to expand the services on offer to the community and to meet government requirements for primary health care. The subsequent expansion of services offered by the new primary health care team raises the relevant question of whether the size of client lists in general practices could be stabilised or even increased. Some general practitioners have argued that with the appropriate support staff a general practitioner could manage a list of 4000 people[5] instead of the present average of 1870.[6]

Today, nurses can be found promoting health not just in the hospital but in the community, in businesses, and in schools. They are in a particularly strong position to empower people to make healthy choices about the way they live their lives, to recognise and treat a whole range of symptoms themselves, and to carry out their own health checks and apply the lessions of prevention. While nurses are an expensive resource—although considerably cheaper than drug treatment—and ultimately a finite resource, their role as educators and facilitators places an infinite resource at the disposal of their clients.

Relationships in the community

Another infinite resource available to all of us is the improvement of the state of people's relationships with each other. The state of our relationships can affect the health of individuals and the communities in which they live and work. The way we relate to our families, our work colleagues, and the community as well as with health care professionals in times of sickness and health can determine our levels of stress. Stress is a major cause of ill health today. It affects the way we think and behave, our quality of life, performance at work, and physical and psychological health.

In considering the long term health of every member of our community, we can employ our imagination and skill to ensure better planning of our homes, towns, and cities. This could benefit some of the most vulnerable people in society—older people, the very young, disabled people, and people who have difficulty in moving about. This requires that every member of the community takes a wider view of citizenship, consulting those people not normally involved in decision making. We need as well to rethink the siting of our communities in relation to known and suspected health hazards and heavy industry.

Even though some of the resources available to meet or stem demand for health care are infinite, our own imaginations and propensity to think up new and more deadly ways of damaging health are also infinite. The results are labelled entertainment. Every decade, new or renamed drugs are abused, as are cigarettes and alcohol, and we constantly devise more and more ingenious ways to sell these products.

A system of explicit rationing involving public decision making as has been explored in Oregon, for example, might well give a low priority to treating these victims of entertainment. Such a system makes the patient responsible rather than bringing to account those who manufacture illness and death or educating people to make healthy choices about their own lives.

But given the current focus of our health services and the popular discontent about the way in which services are rationed now, moves towards explicit rationing are perhaps inevitable. Tough choices will need to be made.

Making choices

How rationing should be achieved is currently occupying the minds of analysts, professionals, and managers everywhere. Indeed, we risk creating a whole new industry around the concept of rationing through conferences, books, and academic papers. We are in grave danger of investing time and money in examining the process rather than ensuring the delivery of effective health care.

To begin with, a moral principle about who gets treated and for what needs to be established. Should people receive the treatment that they "deserve" on the basis of their contribution to society? Or should the distribution of resources ensure the greatest benefit for the greatest number? Or should those with the greatest need receive priority treatment?

As well as a model of rationing by lifestyle, where the provision of health care reflects whether patients have wilfully damaged their health, aspects of these principles have been adapted in a number of models designed to introduce a more rational approach to rationing health care. The quality adjusted life years (QALY) approach has perhaps attracted most attention.

Although I suspect many health care professionals have had difficulty understanding what quality of life has to with economics, let alone understanding how to calculate a unit of health outcome, the debate about QALYs has stimulated discussion about how health outcomes can be measured and the cost effectiveness of various treatments. Clearly, all rationing decisions require this sort of detailed knowledge about effectiveness and cost effectiveness of treatments if they are to make any practical sense.

All rationing criteria raise problems of opposing philosophical principles and priorities, subjectivity, and definitions. But many believe that a set of formal decisions scrutinised by the public is preferable to the informal and covert decisions that currently govern health care decisions about who is treated for what and when.

The Department of Health in the United Kingdom has suggested that district health authorities should work with other groups when setting local priorities, including local people as well as general practitioners and providers and their clinical staff. While health care professionals can advise on technicalities, says the government, only members of the local community can express their joint values with regard to health care.

Experiments in Britain, such as the rapid appraisal method used in south Sefton to find out how health problems were perceived by the community,[7] have shown that the community cannot always be relied on to prioritise essential health requirements. For example, respondents in south Sefton did not list vaccination and immunisation of children as an important health problem. Generally, experiments of this kind in the United Kingdom and in the United States have indicated strongly that priority setting in this way is complex, and the information needed to make rationing decisions is currently inadequate.

Exploring public values by engaging in debate about priorities, health authorities are more able to understand the strength of feeling in the community about priorities and problems. If the public can discuss health care priorities in terms of general improvements rather than specific treatments, purchasers' awareness of local needs could certainly be enhanced. In return, the purchaser would need to be more explicit about which patients with which conditions could really benefit from the range of health services on offer.

In the United Kingdom we are just beginning to address the issue of health outcome. Since the beginning of the year the NHS Management Executive has distributed *Effective Health Care* to provide health authorities with the information to enable them to make decisions about service provision.

With the reform of the National Health Service, the National Research and Development Programme has been established with regional and local initiatives in health care assessment. Although the initiatives have been controversial, more information of this kind is essential if public consultation by purchasers to establish community priorities and rationing decisions are to have any meaning.

Examining the present system

Before adopting any model of rationing, no matter how "rational" it seems and how sophisticated the public consultation exercise, perhaps we should look again at how we currently ration health services. Shortly after the birth of the National Health Service, when it became clear that demand for services was not going to disappear as the backlog of sickness was cleared, it was felt across the political spectrum that queuing for services was fairer than charging for them.

This may still be the case today. If the queue is managed fairly and openly, then joining a waiting list could be seen as at least as fair as many of the alternatives. And if we accept that those who are in pain or particularly anxious have a stronger claim than patients who are inconvenienced by their condition, its defence becomes stronger. This is not, though, the case with the present system, which gives priority to those who have waited the longest.

Of course, the admission of patients to the waiting list depends on the judgment of the health care professional. But in today's internal market, hard and fast judgments made through a rationing model may prove harder to justify because they will almost certainly prove more difficult to hide. Already, the media highlight the plight of patients who have been refused treatment because it is too expensive. Indeed, subsequent diversion of resources from equally deserving patients to those who have hit the headlines has been called rationing by public realtions.[8]

Given the difficulty of finding a basis for rational rationing decisions and of commanding consensus in the community, as well as the potential for catastrophic public relations, we need to consider whether the present system could be re-examined and managed more efficiently and with greater fairness. And we need to consider whether our concerns about the cost of clinical interventions, about meeting the demand for heroic interventions and the technologies that medical science in the hospital setting can offer, will lead us blinkered down the road to rationing without considering the alternatives.

Assuming that the demand for health care is not infinite; that it does not outstrip resources; and that it may not in fact require a huge injection of resources to meet current demand for clinical treatment or to change the focus of our health services, let us look again at some of these alternatives.

Alternatives to rationing
• The demand for health care is not infinite and may not require a huge injection of resources to meet current demand for treatment
• New technologies for less invasive diagnosis and treatment are in many cases more cost effective than traditional methods
• New ways of using existing resources more effectively have been developed—for example, "hospital at home" schemes

Alternatives to rationing

Alongside what Marinker describes as the "tomorrow's world" syndrome, the idea that human mortality and illness are technical problems for which one day we will have a technical solution, new technologies which involve less invasive diagnosis and treatment have been developed—and in many cases these are more cost effective. New ways of using existing resources more effectively have also been developed.

For example, in Britain "hospital at home" schemes which deliver high level intensive nursing in the home for people who would otherwise have to occupy an expensive hospital bed have proved in many places to be satisfactory to nurses and to patients. The service has also helped to reduce waiting lists by increasing patient throughput, facilitating early discharge, and unblocking beds. A hospital at home scheme has been in operation in Peterborough since 1978 and the evaluation has shown not only that patients like the service but that they have more rapid rates of rehabilitation than those patients who have conventional postoperative care in hospital.[9]

Similar schemes are now taking place elsewhere in the United Kingdom, and ultimately all of them aim to prevent certain patients from being admitted to hospital in the first place. In this case the health service is responding to the needs and wishes of the community and using its nursing resources in a cost effective way.

In conclusion, if we accept that rationing is inevitable we accept that cash for health care must remain at an inadequate level, and that clinical and heroic interventions in the hospital setting take precedence over health gain for the wider community. Buying into the burgeoning rationing industry could lead us blinkered into a new health care process without the knowledge to implement it effectively or giving proper consideration to the alternatives. Until we can put hand on heart and state that we have that knowledge, that it is possible to devise an equitable process for priority setting based on sound and just criteria, we have to deny the philosophical basis for rationing.

1 Audit Commission. *Lying in Wait*. London: HMSO, 1992.
2 Flood FD, Diers D. Nurse staffing, patient outcome and cost. *Nursing Management* 1988; **19**: 34–5, 38–9, 42–3.
3 Buchan J, Ball J. *Caring costs: nursing costs and benefits*. Brighton: Institute of Manpower Studies, 1991.
4 Bloor K, Maynard A. *Through the looking glass—opening up the NHS funding debate. A discussion paper*. London: Institute of Health Services Management, 1993.
5 Marsh G. Caring for larger lists. *BMJ* 1991; **303**: 1312–6.
6 Office of Health Economics. *Compendium of Health Statistics 1992*. London: OHE, 1992.
7 Ong BN. Rapid appraisal in an urban setting, an example from the developed world. *Soc Sci Med* 1991; **32**: 909–15.
8 Blank R. *Rationing medicine*. New York: Columbia University Press, 1988.
9 Marks L. *Home and hospital care: re-drawing the boundaries*. London: King's Fund, 1991.

3 Priority setting in the NHS

VIRGINIA BOTTOMLEY

Setting priorities is an issue for any organisation. For an organisation the size of the National Health Service, spending £100 million every 24 hours, it assumes a crucial importance. The process should be sensible; it should be founded on science; it should be based on experience and research. It should take account of actual outcomes. It should be open.

The priorities that the NHS sets itself affect us all—both as people who work with and for the health service and as citizens who rely on it. It is important to take forward a discussion on priorities, engaging as wide a range of groups as possible .

Born in the grim era of postwar rationing, the NHS offered the enticing promise of limitless health care available to all, when and where needed, free at the point of delivery. It was not long before a somewhat different reality presented itself. No government could afford to interpret this promise literally. Bevan resigned from government at the prospect of prescription charges, which was one facet of the priorities debate developing even then.

The need for priority setting has been recognised ever since. Public understanding of the issue has lagged somewhat behind. For that we must all take a share of the blame. The challenge now is to improve that understanding of the choices that always have been and always will be made.

The subject is not new to the NHS, nor is it unique to Britain. Nations all over the world, with a diversity of health care systems and of health care spending, face similar issues. We keep in touch with developments elsewhere. Indeed, we have been active in spreading our experience of health reform to other countries. There have been a number of well publicised approaches to the so called "rationing" debate. Many have heard of the Oregon experiment. Not so many are familiar with the priority setting work in the Netherlands and in New Zealand. These valuable experiences are worth attention.

The scope for priority setting

The approach adopted by Oregon was a brave experiment. On the plus side, it showed the importance of community participation and the central role that must be taken by the medical profession. But my overall conclusion is to agree with the comments of the New Zealand public that the experiment was flawed on administrative, medical, and ethical grounds. In the NHS we neither want nor need Oregon's flawed approach.

Of course, we need to improve the services we provide by better use of the vast resources we have. But, above all, the NHS will continue to offer care on the basis of need, not ability to pay.

That commitment is not negotiable. It is one of the realities of the NHS. Another is that the government will continue to provide the health service with real terms increases in resources year on year. A third is that, notwithstanding that pledge, resources will always be finite. Any discussion must start from these first principles.

What is perhaps different today is our ability to establish and set priorities. With the introduction of the health reforms the process has changed from being implicit to explicit. As a consequence, our readiness to examine how best to set priorities has altered as well. The issue now is how to develop further the skills we need to respond to this challenge.

Framework for priority setting

Priority setting is a task which takes place at every level. We need to be clear about which decisions have to be taken, and where.

First of all, no one should ignore the government's wider duty to establish priorities across all public spending and the economy as a whole. We have to weigh carefully the competing claims of health against education, transport, housing, and many other needs and, no less importantly, what level of taxation it is right to impose on the public.

The task of health ministers is to give strategic direction to the NHS. *The Health of the Nation* is an example of this approach. It identifies five key areas for progress—cancer, coronary heart disease, sexual health, mental illness, and accidents. Similarly, in the Patient's Charter the government has set out rights and standards in key service areas by which the whole NHS must abide. Our recent proposals for London are a further example: policies which are leading to a much needed shift in priority from secondary to primary care.

These are legitimate strategic issues for the government to decide. But that is not the appropriate level at which to take decisions on clinical priority. Those decisions should be taken locally. They must involve managers, consultants, general practitioners, nurses, and the public. They must be made on the basis of sound evidence. Our health reforms have provided a better mechanism for such local decision making.

The process must be led by purchasers. They are now best placed to set priorities intelligently and responsibly, and to reflect the broad spectrum of local needs. Their decisions must be based on delivering national priorities; building a dialogue with the public; using research based evidence based on sound professional advice; and making the best use of resources and pushing value for money.

Doctors and nurses take decisions on priorities in respect of their individual patients every day. There is nothing revolutionary in this. This role carries with it both a challenge and a responsibility, sometimes a heavy one. On top of this onerous duty, professionals also have an important second role: working with the district health authority to help determine broader health priorities. Their skills, understanding, and experience should help ensure that purchasing reflects clinical judgments and is soundly based on clinical knowledge.

A full and informed dialogue between managers, clinicians, and other staff is essential to making purchasing successful. Meeting the health needs of local populations and releasing the enormous potential that exists for better targeting of resources is a job for white coats as well as white collars.

Specifically, understanding the effectiveness of clinical interventions is the key to proper priority setting. And when I talk about

> The wishes of the patient must be given a much higher priority. There are many ways in which we can improve our responsiveness to patients' views. Another challenge to the professions is to make the treatment process more responsive to the needs of the patient.

effectiveness, I mean treatments that take into account the needs of patients, have good outcomes, and represent value for money.

The range and sophistication of the treatments provided by the NHS today reflect the remarkable advances that have been made since its foundation. We now, for example, carry out 45 000 hip replacement operations a year; in 1960 they were not available. Before 1981 the NHS had not performed a single liver transplant; today there are over 400 a year. The number of patients we are treating has expanded enormously. Since 1979 the number of patients the NHS treats annually has risen by over 40%.

The scope of general practice has changed almost beyond recognition. General practitioners are now able to deal with a far greater range of illness than ever before. Significantly, the NHS is now taking on the wider role that it should always have had. Prevention has now taken its proper place alongside treatment and rehabilitation. This has meant additional responsibility for family health services in health promotion and has led to the expansion in activity following up the *Health of the Nation* white paper.

These developments are exciting and valuable. We must continue to develop and promote them where they prove useful. But if we are to do this the NHS—as individual professions, and as an organisation—must continually assess and evaluate the work it does. Only by doing so can priority be given to effective treatments and the ineffective treatments weeded out.

There are potentially enormous gains to be made by identifying better means of achieving improved health for our population. The treatments we provide must prove their worth in three different ways: they must meet the needs of patients; they must be clinically effective—that is, they must have good outcomes and be related to the quality of life; and they must represent value for money.

Patients' views

We need to consider the views of patients on the care they are being offered. If the treatment achieves its clinical outcome only at the cost of disproportionate pain and inconvenience to the patient, can you say that you have achieved a successful outcome? The Patient's Charter makes it clear: the wishes of the patient must be given a much higher priority.

Patients generally prefer less intensive, less invasive surgery. They are keen to spend less time away from their homes and work. There are many ways in which we can improve our responsiveness to patients' views. To give one example, the Central Middlesex Hospital, with the support of the King's Fund, is running a trial of an interactive video for patients considering prostatectomies. This gives them basic information on the risks and benefits of the operation. Trials of this kind can show that well informed patients often make different decisions from clinicians.

I agree with the medical profession that treatment should be a partnership between clinicians and patients. So, another challenge to the professions is to make the treatment process more responsive to the needs of the patient. How can you engage the public more, and improve their understanding of the treatment they are offered?

Clinical effectiveness

Before we can be confident that we are using resources appropriately, we need to have a much better knowledge of the outcomes of clinical interventions. Treatments that were previously common have been shown to be either ineffective or overused—for example, grommets or tonsillectomies. At the same time, we need to understand more clearly the health gain that can be obtained from different procedures—for example, hip replacements or medical treatments for leukaemia.

We have started on this road. Medical and clinical audit have laid the foundations for a much better understanding by both doctors and nurses of the outcome of their treatments. The clinical effectiveness bulletins and the Central Health Outcomes Unit are sources of information on existing knowledge on effectiveness.

This work will increasingly be informed and underpinned by the NHS research and development strategy, launched in 1991 and led by Professor Michael Peckham. One of the key planks of this strategy is the expansion of what is known as health technology assessment—that is, the assessment of effectiveness, cost, and the broader impact of health care in interventions.

Producing valid, research based information on the vast array of interventions now confronting those purchasing and providing health care is a daunting task. This is why the research and development strategy itself places emphasis on identifying research priorities for the NHS to ensure that research and development resources are applied to areas where the NHS can most benefit from the information derived.

When we do have information on effectiveness we must ensure that it is being properly used in routine practice, in the right way and on the right patients. That is why medical and clinical audit are so vital.

Most importantly, the chief medical officer and the chief nursing officer have recently set up the Clinical Outcomes Group to bring practising clinicians from a range of professions together with managers to develop our understanding of this crucial area. This knowledge and information must be used to inform purchasing.

There is more we can do in this field. The rewards are potentially vast. Another challenge for today should be how the medical and nursing professions can work with the other health professionals to improve our understanding of outcomes and of effectiveness.

Cost effectiveness

We must consider cost as well as clinical effectiveness. Although we must not compromise the principles on which the NHS provides care, we must search relentlessly for ways of achieving better outcomes and improving health gain, while providing better value for the taxpayers' money.

If a treatment offers substantial health gain at a reasonable cost we must not hesitate to use it. For example, for £4 the NHS can immunise one child for a lifetime against measles, mumps, and rubella. That represents good health value. When we looked at breast cancer screening in the Forrest report[2] it was clear that we could save over 1000 lives each year by screening women aged 50–64 years, at a cost of £55 million. That also represents good health value.

Where there is a cheaper way of dealing effectively with the same ailment, the NHS has a responsibility to use it, to release savings for other areas of health care. The use of cheaper drugs, of the same quality and efficacy, can save the health service millions of pounds. We should also recognise that it is not the case that

> ## Challenges in priority setting
> - Improve understanding of choices that have been and always will be made
> - Make the treatment process more responsive to the needs of the patient
> - Produce valid, research based information on interventions
> - Ensure that information on effectiveness is being properly used in routine practice
> - Medical and nursing professions working with other health professionals to improve understanding of outcomes and of effectiveness
> - Achieve better outcomes and improve health gain while providing better value for taxpayers' money
> - Increase understanding of cost effectiveness
> - Accelerate the development of clinical guidelines

medical advances always lead to more costs. By taking advantage of the developments in minimally invasive surgery to reduce length of stay, for example, the NHS can continue to make more treatments available in other areas. We can do a great deal more to improve our understanding in this area.

This poses the next challenge: how can we increase our understanding of cost effectiveness? For example, should all health technology be assessed before it passes into the NHS? Should drug companies be required to provide evidence on the cost effectiveness of their products before release onto the market?

Clinical guidelines

Clinical guidelines offer a sensible way of reflecting the values I have discussed in the treatment of patients. They form a basis for agreement between local clinicians and management. Good clinical guidelines should reflect all three criteria: views of patients, clinical effectiveness, and cost effectiveness. There is another challenge here: how can we accelerate the development of clinical guidelines?

Conclusion

One of the biggest challenges to the professions over the coming years is how we can ensure the priorities are set sensibly at local level, with regard to the needs of the patient and on the basis of

> Decisions on clinical priority should be taken locally. The process
> must be led by purchasers, whose decisions must be based on
> - Delivering national priorities
> - Building a dialogue with the public
> - Using evidence based on research and on sound professional
>   advice
> - Making the best use of resources and pushing value for money

sound information on cost and outcome. This is one of the greatest
challenges to the profession over the coming years. The debate
should not be confused with the issue of how much money should
be devoted to the NHS. That is a legitimate question, but a
different one. We are talking about how we make the best possible
use of the NHS resources, whatever their level.

The discussion takes place against a background of an aging
population and growing expectations, and with the potential to
heal pushed to ever greater limits by new technology. Politicians
are taught early on to talk about challenges rather than problems.
However, none of us should buy in to the fashionable theory that
the NHS is rushing towards some sort of rationing armageddon.
Sensible practitioners and politicians have known all along that
hard decisions about priorities have to be taken.

We have been taking those decisions all the time, perhaps
without even realising it. On the whole we have been getting it
right. Why else should, every year, the NHS produce so many
millions of satisfied customers? It would be a shame if, now that we
are talking openly about the subject, we suddenly lose sight of this
wider perspective.

1. Secretary of State for Health. *The health of the nation: a strategy for health in England.*
   London: HMSO, 1992. (SM 1986.)
2. Working Group on Breast Cancer Screening. *Report to the Health Ministers of England,
   Wales, Scotland and Northern Ireland.* London: HMSO, 1986. (Professor Sir Patrick
   Forrest, chairman.)

PART II: PRACTICAL EXPERIENCE

4 Prioritising health services in an era of limits: the Oregon experience

JOHN A KITZHABER

As we approach the end of the twentieth century, health care systems around the world are struggling with the dual problems of cost and access. Although there are vast differences between the British system and the American system—and between these systems and those in Canada, Germany, or New Zealand—there is a central issue shared by all nations: what are we buying with our health care dollars and what is the relationship between these expenditures and health?

As populations age and technology expands, the cost of health care rises. At the same time we find ourselves facing the need for increased investments in education, in infrastructure, in transportation systems, and in addressing a host of other pressing social problems such as environmental pollution, crime, and substance abuse. The competition for limited public resources between these diverse needs means that we can no longer afford to do everything that medical science has to offer for everyone who might benefit from it. In short, we must set priorities. The question is, how do we decide?

In this chapter I will examine how this question was answered in the state of Oregon. My purpose is not to convince you of the merits of the Oregon process, nor to draw any conclusions about its possible relevance to the United Kingdom. Rather, my purpose is to describe our experience as objectively as I can and to share what insights I have gained through the experience from my dual perspective as an American politician and a primary care physician.

35

Oregon's health plan is based on publicly debated priorities

Framework for health care reform

Health care reform can be viewed as a debate over how to answer three questions—Who is covered? What is covered? How is it financed and delivered?—asked in the context of an ultimate objective. (This framework is drawn from Aristotle's "teleologic" view of change, according to which change (or reform) must be driven by a clear objective, or final cause, and by three subsidiary factors: the material cause, the formal cause, and the efficient cause.) Successful reform, then, must start with consensus on a clearly articulated objective and must explicitly answer these three questions in a way that is consistent with that objective.

The need for consensus on an objective may sound obvious, but consider the current national health care reform debate in the United States, where the objective seems to be to reduce cost, to improve access, or both. But is reducing cost really the end or is it the means to an end? Why do we want to reduce costs? Because cost is a major barrier to access. Why do we want people to have access to health care? Because we want people to be healthy, which is important to individuals and to our society. Thus, both reducing costs and improving access are actually means to an end—the end, or objective, being to improve, maintain, or restore health. I will elaborate further on this point later.

Who is covered?

Now let us turn to the three questions. The first question—"who is covered?" is not really at issue—or at least is not particularly controversial. Currently in the United Kingdom, for example, or in Canada, or New Zealand, the answer to this question is "everyone." These countries have developed systems in which virtually all citizens have coverage for some level of health care: universal coverage—with eligibility based generally on citizenship.

The United States, however, has never had a national policy of universal coverage. In fact, eligibility for coverage under the two major government financed programmes, Medicaid and Medicare, is based not on citizenship but rather on category. These two programmes were enacted in 1965 in reaction to President Johnson's Task Force on Health, which reported that elderly people and children in low income families faced the greatest financial barriers to access to good health services. The task force recommended that Congress expand maternal and child health programmes for the poor and enact publicly financed hospital insurance for the elderly. Thus the objective was not universal coverage but rather coverage only for those interest groups or "categories" which, in 1965, were perceived to have the greatest difficulty gaining access to the system.

As a result Medicaid is a programme that provides all "medically necessary" services to certain "categories" of poor people but not to all poor people. To be eligible one must fit into a congressionally designated "category" such as families with dependent children or the blind or disabled. Just being poor is not enough. Poor men and women without children, for example, are ineligible even though they may be deeply impoverished. In other words, the United States has developed a system that makes an artificial distinction between the "deserving poor" (those who fit into a category) and the "undeserving poor" (those who don't). Medicare, on the other hand, is a federally administered "entitlement" programme for those in the category over the age of 65. It is not means tested, so everyone over the age of 65 receives publicly subsidised health care regardless of whether they retire in poverty or on $2 million a year.

Under this categorical approach to eligibility wealthy retired citizens, such as former presidents Jimmy Carter and Ronald Reagan, are entitled to publicly subsidised health care that is paid for in part by the tax contributions of working poor citizens who have none. Under this system, millionaires over the age of 65 are entitled to coverage for all the latest medical technology while poor childless women are entitled to no coverage whatsoever—not even for basic preventive care of proved effectiveness—until or unless they become pregnant.

Coverage for what?

Due in large part to these gross inequities, there is broad and growing consensus in the United States that universal coverage for some level of health care must be a central part of reform. For that reason, most of the current debate revolves around the third question, how is it financed and delivered? The debate over global budgets and managed competition, over "pay or play" mechanisms or a single payer system—all are variations on the answer to this question. The crucial question of what is covered, however, goes largely unaddressed.

In the United Kingdom the issue of priority setting in the National Health Service is an attempt to come to terms with the question of what is covered. Answering this question is the fundamental common challenge of health care systems around the world. The United Kingdom has a system of universal coverage but in order to afford it people are beginning to ask themselves what they are buying for their health care money and what the relation is between those expenditures and health. In the United States, although the current administration continues to shy away from this issue, it is clear that to achieve universal coverage we must ultimately come to terms with the question of "coverage for what?"

Hospitalisation only? prescription drugs? immunisations? organ transplants? new technologies? experimental procedures? facelifts? liposuction? sex change operations? everything? nothing? Is it significant that advocates for reform are very vague on this issue. We hear such words as "comprehensive" or "basic" or "medically necessary," but nowhere do we hear a definitive explanation of exactly what that means in terms of real health services. President Clinton has promised to provide all Americans access to a "basic" level of health care, but he has not defined exactly what constitutes "basic" care, nor has he outlined a process by which it can be clarified.

Unless we define basic care as "everything for anyone who might possibly benefit from it"—which is incompatible with both deficit reduction and making other important social investments, some of which also affect health—then some difficult choices will have to be made. And of course we are reluctant to take this step because when we define what constitutes basic care we must also define what is not basic, and I can tell you from personal experience that confronting this issue is very controversial. Yet to avoid it is to continue the futile debate over how to pay for "something" for "someone," which is like debating the budget for a banquet for which there is no defined menu and no guest list.

We are reluctant to come to terms with this issue, at least in the United States, because, although we are unwilling (and increasingly unable) to pay for everything, we are also unwilling to set limits. Not only is setting limits politically unpopular, in the process of doing so—in the process of determining the level of care to which all citizens will have access—society must come to terms with the relationship between the provision of health care and the pursuit of health; with the relative effectiveness and appropriateness of medical services and procedures; with issues of administrative costs and medicolegal liability; with issues of social expectations and individual responsibility; and with a host of difficult moral and ethical questions.

Clearly, the questions of what is covered is the most difficult, the most controversial, and yet perhaps the most important of the three. It is the sine qua non of lasting health care reform, and for that reason there must be a process by which it can be answered—a process that involves the public, is linked to the reality of fiscal limits, and has clear lines of accountability.

Setting Oregon's objectives

As I mentioned earlier, to answer meaningfully the three questions of who is covered, what is covered and how it is financed and delivered, there must first be consensus on the objective. Reaching broad based consensus on the objective was the starting point of the Oregon Health Plan. We asked ourselves whether the objective was to give all Oregonians access to health care, or to keep Oregonians healthy. We determined that the objective must be health—not universal coverage, not access to health care, not cost containment, but rather, health. Health care is a means to an end, not an end in itself—that is, health care is not necessarily synonymous with health.

Infant mortality, for example, reflects more than just a lack of prenatal health care. It also reflect housing problems, environmental problems, teenage pregnancies, and the growing problem of substance abuse. The point is that we cannot achieve the objective of health as long as we spend money only on the medical complications of substance abuse, yet ignore the social conditions that lead to addiction in the first place. And that means having the budgetary flexibility to invest in such things as housing, education, and economic opportunity.

Beyond that, it should also be clear that medical procedures are not of equal value and effectiveness in producing health. For example, nearly half of the Medicare budget is spent on the last few months of life and it is estimated that well over half of the costs of intensive care units are expended on non-survivors. By no stretch of the imagination could these expenditures be said to be effective or to produce health. Too often they merely prolong the process of dying.

Thus, the primary objective of health care reform efforts must be to develop not merely a strategy to purchase health care, but rather a health policy—an integrated approach in which expenditures for health care are balanced with expenditures in related areas which also affect health. In addition there must be some criteria by which to ensure that the expenditures we make for health care actually produce health.

Let us assume, for the purpose of argument, that we agree on a policy objective of health. This means that the three questions must be answered in a way that maintains, improves or restores health. The Oregon Health Plan represents a process and a framework by which this could be and was accomplished (box 1). As I describe this process, I will touch only briefly on how we answered the questions of who is covered and how health care is financed and delivered; I will focus most of my attention on the question of priority setting—on answering the central question of what is covered.

Box 1—The Oregon Health Plan

Objective:	*Health*
Who is covered?	Everyone (universal access)
What is covered?	Uniform basic benefit
How is it financed?	Public and private partnership

Who is covered? How is it financed?

To the question "who is covered" Oregon answered "everyone" since access to some level of health care is clearly necessary to achieve the objective of health. Universal coverage was accomplished through the enactment of two bills in 1989. Senate Bill 27 extended eligibility for Medicaid to all those with a family income below the federal poverty level ($991 a month for a family of three). Senate Bill 935 mandated comparable employment based coverage for full time workers and their dependants with family incomes above the federal poverty level. That is, we expanded the role of government in subsidising care for the poor and built on our existing employment based system of coverage. (As currently written the Oregon Health Plan will provide coverage for 95% of Oregonians under the age of 65 (those over 65 are covered by Medicare). It misses part time workers with incomes above the federal poverty level and seasonal workers, who may spend part of the year outside the state.)

Thus, to the question of how is it financed, Oregon answered: "through a public-private partnership." Society, through general tax revenues, was responsible for those without the ability to pay, while those with incomes above the federal poverty level would receive workplace based coverage with the costs split between the employer and the employee.

What is covered?

The move toward universal coverage (a policy Great Britain has already achieved) shifted the debate from "who is covered?" to "what is covered?" To answer the question of "what is covered?" in Oregon, a Health Services Commission was created, consisting of five primary care physicians, a public health nurse, a social

41

worker, and four consumers. The members were appointed by the governor and confirmed by the senate after public hearings. The commission was charged with developing a "list of health services ranked in priority from the most important to the least important, according to the comparative benefits of each service to the entire population being served" and judged by a consideration of clinical effectiveness and social values.

To carry out the requirement to consider clinical effectiveness, the commission used medical "condition-treatment pairs" gleaned from two widely recognised classifications of diagnosis and treatment, the Current Procedural Technology (the CPT-4 codes) and the International Classification of Diseases (the ICD-9 codes). Examples of condition-treatment pairs are appendicectomy for acute apppendicitis, antibiotics for bacterial pneumonia, and bone marrow transplant for leukaemia. The initial list of nearly 3000 pairs was substantially reduced by combining those for which treatment and outcome were essentially the same. For example, there are multiple codes to describe various kinds of uncomplicated fractures of the long bones of the upper arm. Since the treatment for such fractures is essentially the same, and since outcomes are similar, these codes were consolidated into a single condition-treatment pair. By this process the list was reduced to around 1000 pairs.

The determination of clinical effectiveness was based on the input of panels of physicians, who were asked to provide certain clinical information about each condition-treatment pair in their areas of practice. Over 7000 hours of volunteer time was given by Oregon physicians to this effort. We recognise that much of this information represents a consensus by physicians rather than hard empirical outcomes data. None the less, it provided a snapshot on how medicine was currently being practised in Oregon and offered a starting point and a rational framework in which better information on outcomes could be integrated as it became available. It is also important to note that the prioritisation process is dynamic and ongoing. That is, a new priority list is generated each budget cycle to take into consideration new technologies and new information on outcomes.

In addition to considering clinical effectiveness, the commission set up a broad based public process to identify and attempt to integrate social values into the priority list. The statute specified that this public involvement take three forms. Firstly, the commission was required to "actively solicit public involvement in a community meeting process to build a consensus on the values to be used to guide health resources allocation decisions." Secondly, the commission was required to hold a series of public hearings around the state and to solicit "testimony and information" from a full range of health care systems including all recognised advocacy groups for various populations and illnesses and all recognised health care providers. Finally, the legislation required that the Health Services Commission and all of its proceedings be subject to full public disclosure under Oregon's open meetings laws, which govern public bodies.

Involving the public

The Health Services Commission, aware of the importance of public involvement to the success of its work, went well beyond the outreach process required by the legislature. It immediately contacted the various health care interest groups in the state (especially advocates for the poor, the uninsured, and for consumers in general) and enlisted their assistance in generating public participation. By encouraging attendance at Health Service Commission meetings and hearings, and by soliciting testimony, we sought to ensure that the commission received input and information from the broadest possible citizen base. While it is clear that our initial efforts to involve a representative cross section of citizens can and must be improved, the level of public participation in the commission's work was unprecedented, even in a state that prides itself on open and accessible government.

To fulfil the legislative requirement for a community meeting process, the commission turned to Oregon Health Decisions, a grassroots bioethics organisation founded in 1983 by Ralph Crawshaw, a Portland psychiatrist, and Michael Garland, an ethicist at the Oregon Health Sciences University. Dedicated to educating Oregonians on the health policy choices confronting them and on the consequences of these choices, Oregon Health Decisions had been conducting community discussions on a variety of ethical issues for nearly 10 years. Under the auspices of this group the Health Services Commission organised the most extensive town hall meeting process ever conducted in the state. The initial objective was to have at least one town hall meeting in each of

Box 2—High ranking priorities

- Acute, fatal conditions where treatment prevents death and leads to full recovery
- Maternity care
- Acute, fatal conditions where treatment prevents death but does not lead to full recovery
- Preventive care for children
- Chronic, fatal conditions where treatment prolongs life and improves its quality
- Comfort care

Oregon's 36 counties. Not only was that objective met but multiple sessions were conducted in more densely populated areas, bringing the total number of town hall meetings to 47.

After the meetings were completed, the results and opinions of the participants were tabulated and assembled into a report for use by the Health Services Commission and the legislature. The resulting document, *Health Care in Common*, was used extensively by the Health Services Commission in its deliberations and stands as an exceptional example of constructive activism by a dedicated group of citizens.

The first priority list, completed in February 1991, consists of 709 condition-treatment pairs divided into 17 categories. The priority of the categories is based on the commission's interpretation of the social values generated from the public involvement process. Within each category the ranking of the condition-treatment pairs reflects the benefit likely to result from each procedure and the duration of the benefit. (Mental health and chemical dependency services as well as physical health services are included in the plan; a somewhat different priority setting process was needed for chemical dependency services.)

Services in the highest category were those for acute, fatal conditions where treatment prevents death and returns the individual to his or her previous health state (such as an appendicectomy for appendicitis) (box 2). Because of the high value placed on prevention by those participating in the community outreach process, the categories of maternity care (including prenatal, natal, and postpartum care) and of preventive care for children ranked very high. Also ranked high as a direct result of the outreach process were dental care and hospice care. At the bottom of the list

> ## Box 3—Results of the Oregon Health Plan's process
> - Recognition of fiscal units
> - Universal coverage
> - Health policy
> - Clear accountability
> - Consensus definition of "basic care"

were categories of services for minor conditions, futile care, and services that had little or no effect on health status.

The final priority list was given to an independent actuarial firm, which determined the cost of delivering each element on the list through capitated managed care. The list and its accompanying actuarial data were given to the legislature on 1 May 1991.

Results of the process

Since the legislature is statutorily prohibited from altering the order of the priorities as established by the Health Services Commission, it was required to start at the top of the list and determine how much could be funded from available revenues and what additional revenues would be needed to fund an acceptable "basic" package (box 3). In this way, the question "what is covered?" was directly linked to the reality of fiscal limits.

Furthermore, since the state could no longer arbitrarily "ration people" for reasons of budgetary expediency, everyone retained coverage (universal coverage) and the debate centred on the level of that coverage: on the answer to the critical question, "what is covered?"—on what we as a society are willing to fund, and thus guarantee, to all of our citizens.

Because of Oregon's constitutional requirement for a balanced budget, it was clear that increases in the health care budget must come at the expense of other programmes such as education or corrections. This enabled the legislature to begin to develop an overall health policy which recognises that health can be maintained only if investments in several related areas are balanced.

Finally, because of the list and the explicit nature of the process, the legislature is clearly and inescapably accountable not just for what it funds in the health care budget but also for what it chooses not to fund. This kind of accountability is a major departure from the current system.

45

> ## Box 4—Consensus definition of basic care
> - Initial evaluation and diagnosis
> - All preventive and screening services
> - Dental services
> - Hospice care
> - Prescription drugs
> - Routine physical examinations
> - Mammography
> - Most transplants
> - Physical and occupational therapy
> - Virtually all Medicaid mandates

As a result of this accountable and explicit process the 1991 Oregon legislature reached consensus on the definition of basic care by appropriating $33 million in new revenue, which funded all condition-treatment pairs through line 587 on the list of 709. The resulting benefit package, with its strong emphasis on primary and preventive care, is eminently defensible (box 4). It covers the initial evaluation and diagnosis for all conditions, virtually all current Medicaid mandates, including all preventive and screening services, as well as a number of important services not required by Medicaid, including dental services, hospice care, prescription drugs, routine physicals, mammography, most transplants, and physical and occupational therapy. (Because the prioritisation process is dynamic and ongoing, a new list was submitted to the 1993 legislature. This second list consists of 696 line items. In August 1993 the legislature funded the new list to achieve a benefit level equivalent to that originally funded by the 1991 legislature.

It is important to recognise that the benefit package we have funded serves as the minimum standard not only for the Medicaid programme but also for the 360 000 Oregonians who will come into the system on the employer side by 1995. By then the package will become the standard benefit offered by all private policies in the state. To fully implement the establishment of this statewide "floor" will require affirmative action by the legislature in 1995 as well as additional federal waivers.

Finally, the Oregon Health Plan includes a "liability shield" for providers—a statutory distinction between actual medical malpractice and not providing a service that society has determined not to fund. This will help reduce defensive medicine and will allow society, not the courts, to determine the level of care it wishes to guarantee to all of its citizens. Furthermore, it will allow the development and actual implementation of practice standards without substantially increasing the risk of medical malpractice suits. Perhaps most importantly, however, it will allow health care providers to continue to be patient advocates within the context of the resources society has made available.

This then, is the Oregon Health Plan. On 19 March 1993 the Clinton administration granted Oregon the federal waivers necessary to proceed with implementation. At the time of writing, the Oregon legislature was in the process of funding the new priority list, and the programme is expected to be operational by 1 January 1994.

Conclusion

Although viewed as controversial outside the state, the plan was enacted with broad based support. It was not achieved through confrontation nor by trying to find villains and scapegoats. Rather, it represents a consensus building exercise that was supported by the Oregon Medical Association, the Association of Oregon Hospitals, consumer groups, organised labour, and the business community. It passed both houses of the Oregon legislature with huge majorities in both parties.

Our success was due in large part to our willingness to challenge openly two of the underlying assumptions of the current American health care system: that health care is synonymous with health and that all medical services are of equal value and effectiveness. We may pretend that this is not so, but as Thomas Henry Huxley pointed out, "Facts do not cease to exist just because we choose to ignore them." The fact is that we have become obsessed with the delivery of health care rather than with the pursuit of health. It may be controversial and politically unpopular to reduce "benefits," but if by benefit we mean something that maintains, restores, or improves health then much of what we currently spend our health care budget on would not qualify as benefits and could therefore be eliminated without "rationing" health care and without adversely affecting health.

As I stated at the beginning of this paper, it has not been my purpose to convince you of the merits of the Oregon process nor to draw any conclusions about its possible relevance to the United

Kingdom. I believe, however, that ultimately Britain too must explicitly answer the question of what is covered. Whether this answer is arrived at through a process such as the one we used in Oregon or by some other means is not important—what is important is that it be done. And if there is one thing we have shown in Oregon, it is that it can be done—through a process which brings the public and the medical community together in common cause to work for the common good.

Copies of *Health Care in Common* can be purchased from Oregon Health Decisions, 921 SW Washington (Suite 723), Portland, Oregon 97205. Copies of the priority list and of the report of the Health Services Commission can be purchased from the Office of Medical Assistance Programs, Writer's Group, 500 Summer NE, Salem, Oregon 97310-1014.

5 Dutch choices in health care

RLJM SCHEERDER

The Dutch healthcare system has been in the process of change since the middle of the 1980s. From 1987 onwards this process was strengthened by the reform plans of the Dekker committee and later by the plan of the present minister of health, Hans Simons. This restructuring has stimulated debate on priority setting in health care, or choices in health care, from the perspective of social health insurance.

The present financing system

Financing of health care in the Netherlands is primarily based on an insurance system. It is important to know something of the system to understand the Dutch debate on choices in health care. Apart from a limited government subsidy system in certain areas, there are three main insurance systems for health care.

Exceptional Medical Expenses Act

The Exceptional Medical Expenses Act is a national insurance scheme and covers the 15 million people resident in the Netherlands. The insurance is statutory: everyone meeting the criteria is insured and must pay the relevant contribution.

The treatment and services available under this act are mainly the following: nursing homes, psychiatric care, care for disabled and mentally handicapped people, services of a home care organisation, pharmaceutical care.

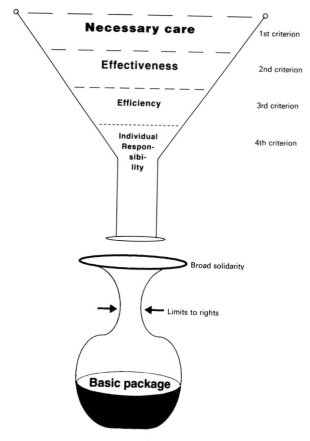

Treatments and services in the basic package form a funnel with four sieves—certain types of care will be retained while others fall through into the basic package

The cost of this insurance is covered mainly by income-related contributions; there is a small, flat rate premium and a relatively small government fund.

Health Insurance Act

Insurance under the Health Insurance Act is statutory: everyone meeting the criteria is insured. This scheme covers about nine million people, mainly working people whose annual income is below about 55 000 guilders. It also extends to the recipients of social security benefits up to the age of 65 and a specified group of people over 65.

Transforming health care in the Netherlands

The situation now...
- Exceptional Expenses Act
- Health Insurance Act
- Private insurance
- Civil service schemes

...and when change is complete
- Basic insurance
- Additional private schemes

Medical and surgical treatment, dental care, obstretic care, hospital residence, transport, and maternity care are available under this act. The cost of this scheme is mainly covered by income related premiums and a relatively small flat rate contribution and government grant.

Private Insurance

The private health insurance schemes are carried out by private companies: profit or non-profit organisations, often in alliance with the sick fund organisations, who are responsible for the execution of the Health Insurance Act. They serve about six million people who are insured by the Health Insurance Act, but the private schemes are not compulsory. Their coverage is about the same as that under the Health Insurance Act. The private system does not include the treatments and services of the Exceptional Medical Expenses Act, which covers all residents of the Netherlands.

In the private system there is more freedom of choice in the level of risk accepted and in certain variations in coverage. By choosing a high own risk or excluding certain services from the coverage, people can obtain a reduction in the premium; a lower own risk results in a higher premium. It depends on the individual's perceived level of risk. The cost of the private schemes is covered by flat rate contributions. For civil servants there is a mixed system, which is part of the terms of employment. The premium and coverage for certain groups, such as people over 65, have been determined by legislation.

Changes in the system

The health insurance system is in a state of flux. The plans to amend the system are based on achieving a balance between equality and accessibility on the one hand and market oriented financial incentives on the other hand.

It is seen to be important to integrate health care and related social services; to strengthen efficiency, flexibility, and substitution; and to reduce the role of government, giving way to the parties concerned: insurers, providers, and patients. The Cabinet proposes to introduce gradually one basic insurance system for all residents; shift financial and planning responsibility from government to health care providers and insurers; deregulate or abolish the existing health insurance acts; and provide more "choices" and financial responsibilities for individual patients.

In this transformation process the political and public debate is focused on the final insurance coverage. Hence, discussions on priority setting and choices in health care are very relevant.

The Dunning report

The Dunning committee (the Committee on Choices in Health Care) was instituted by the government in 1990. It was to examine how to put limits on new technologies, deal with scarcity, and ration care, and to propose strategies to improve choices in health care on different levels.

The Dunning report dealt with many aspects and had great impact in the Netherlands, making an important contribution to the political and public debate.[1] I shall concentrate on two main points of the report: its approach toward the choices debate, and the impact of the debate on choices on developing the basic insurance scheme.

The report's approach

The Dunning report stated that, since choices are necessary, the health care need must be described. Health care needs to maintain or restore health, to care for and nurse injured health, or to relieve suffering. The committee defined health as the ability to function normally. A need for health care is then related to the threat of restricting this functioning. Normal functioning, however, can be defined from three perspectives: those of the individual, medical professionals, and the community.

The individual approach links health to self determination and autonomy. It is the balance between what a person wants and what a person can achieve. This means that the definition varies greatly from person to person and an overall definition must be very broad. Letting individuals decide on what they need would prevent a community definition of necessary care.

The medical professional approach defines health as the absence of disease. The effectiveness of care is defined objectively, with the most important criterion being danger to life and the extent of normal biological function. This definition neglects the psychosocial functioning of individuals and their social circumstances.

In the community approach, health is the possibility for every member of the community to function as normally as possible. Priorities are community oriented, so necessary care includes homes for elderly people, care for mentally handicapped people, etc—in short, a system based on consensus. This was the approach chosen by the Dunning committee.

The Dunning system of priorities

The Dunning committee developed a strategy for making choices in health care according to the community approach. It focused its strategy on deciding the contents of the coverage of basic social health insurance. The treatments and services in the basic package should satisfy four criteria, forming as it were a funnel with four sieves (figure) in which certain types of care will be retained while others fall through.

The first sieve retains care that is not necessary according to the community approach. The second sieve selects on the basis of effectiveness; only care for which the effectiveness has been confirmed and documented belongs in the basic package. The third sieve selects on the basis of efficiency, using cost effectiveness and cost utility analysis. The fourth sieve retains care that may be left to individual responsibility and individual payment.

The committee gave several examples to illustrate how this strategy works. For instance, dental care for adults can be left out of the basic package; good dental care and prevention for the young people make it possible to leave dental care to adults' individual responsibilities. Another example is the question of the position of homoeopathic medicines in the basic insurance package. On the basis of the effectiveness and efficiency criteria the committee came to the conclusion that these medicines should be left up to the individual and should not be part of the basic insurance.

53

Barriers to improving quality of health care

1 History taking and physical examination should remain pivotal in medical practice, followed by additional diagnostic testing. Inappropriate use of diagnostic tests is increasing; overuse, as well as underuse, occurs.

2 The current fee for service payment undervalues history taking, talking with patients, and physical examination while it favours diagnostic testing.

3 The scarcity of data concerning the effectiveness of diagnosis and treatment is a major obstacle for quality assessment and designing of protocols. A number of procedures have been introduced without proof of their merit.

4 Seldom used and complex procedures should be offered in only a few centres, rather than be widely available. However, plans for centralisation are frequently interfered with by the (financial) interests of hospitals and specialists.

5 Not all doctors attend postgraduate medical training programmes offered by their professional associations.

6 Patients are making greater demands on their doctors, thus becoming consumers of medical services.

7 Accountability and peer review are not yet routine among practitioners.

8 Collaboration between colleagues leaves something to be desired. Most general practitioners practice alone; group practices of specialists (partnerships) are generally focused on practice organisation rather than development of a common approach to patient management. Specialists and general practitioners do not always cooperate fully.

9 Specialists who use the same technologies come into conflict about who is allowed to do what. Problems also arise when different specialists treat patients with similar disorders differently. Discussions concerning these kinds of "territorial conflicts" tend to concentrate on the interests of the specialty rather than on the wellbeing of the patient.

The Health Council report

At about the time the Dunning report was published, the Dutch Health Council published a report on the position, efficiency, and quality of medical professionals according to the criteria of appropriate use of medical resources, interventions, methods, and applications. The committee attempted to point out the often irrational barriers to quality improvement, which have so far impeded progress in effecting changes. Several examples from the report are shown in the box.

Conclusions and recommendations

The committee concluded that a clear choice by the medical profession was urgently needed, but changing the attitude of the medical profession would take time and patience. Physicians would need the support of their environment: hospital management, patients, and politicians—in a broad sense, of society as a whole.

Improvement of medical practice was primarily a responsibility of the professional group itself. The committee recommended that the scientific board of each specialty should set up its own independent quality assurance commission.

Accountability and systemic evaluation of medical practice should become routine. The committee suggested that the quality assurance commissions develop a procedure for medical audit for all specialist partnerships and general practitioner groups.

Evaluation of the results of rare and complex procedures should get priority. Should this show centralisation to be needed, hospital budgets should be reallocated accordingly.

On the basis of effectiveness research the profession should design protocols for good medical practice in particular circumstances. These should not be applied as strict rules but as guidelines for medical practice.

The committee also recommended changing the remuneration system so that good medical practice would be rewarded; this would have the greatest beneficial effect on quality of care, regardless of which health care system is chosen in the future.

New technologies should be adopted only if their effectiveness has been proved. All new technologies should undergo proper evaluation.

The committee rejected the solitary work style and applauded the government stimulus to group formation for general practitioners. Specialists also should reorganise their work and establish group practices. It is of great importance that general practitioners and specialists realise that cooperation, rather than competition, will improve the quality of patient care.

The ongoing subspecialisation necessitates structured collaboration between specialists in different disciplines, locally, to organise the multidisciplinary treatment of individual patients, and nationally to outline specialised tasks and responsibilities. Patients need an adviser to guide them through the web of specialties.

Improving the status of general practitioners was emphasised so that they would be in a good position to advise patients when important decisions have to be made. It is the family doctor who has the overall picture, particularly when the patient is under treatment by several (sub)specialists at the same time.

The basic medical curriculum and the training of residents should be altered to meet changing standards. It is desirable that epidemiological thinking should become part of the programme from the beginning.

The committee thought that the government should not be too passive. Government intervention is desirable with regard to planning the number of specialists needed and to reallocating hospital budgets when facilities are to be centralised. The committee recommended that rigid regulations should govern the acceptance of new technologies and that government policy continue to be applied.

The government's approach

Although the government endorses the conclusions of the two reports, things are not that easy. The four criteria of the Dunning report seem to be transparent and easy, but they are open to many subjective opinions. What is necessary, for instance? What can be counted as being the individual's responsibility; who is going to decide what you can afford and what you can't? The recommendations of the Health Council report have been stated before, and yet there is still a great overuse of diagnostic and therapeutic actions, and these vary hugely among doctors.

The government has taken serious action in establishing a public debate on health care. Specific funds have been devoted to that debate so as to accommodate political decisions in, for instance, rationing health care and increasing financial responsibilities.

The government is also trying to keep up the debate among the professionals and the managers of institutions and to actively promote the participation of professionals in management. It is deliberately seeking action on all aspects of the health care business, involving all participants: providers, professionals, insurers, private and social institutions, and of course the patient/consumer.

The government is not refraining from using financial incentives to reach the objectives: changes in the tariff systems and in the budget systems, own risk and contributions from patients and insured people.

Specific actions in government policy

Specific measures are being considered to reduce the social insurance package—for instance, not covering dental care for adults, restricting family care in case of the delivery of a child, discontinuing coverage of drugs. Fertility techniques like in vitro fertilisation are being debated, as is the place of contraceptives and abortion in the package.

The process of changing the legislation for the social health package implies simplifying the terms and making it more functional. This will reduce the monopolies of established institutions and make the system more flexible. People can choose alternative health care provisions, which may be cheaper and more efffective, and insurers will have more possibilities to make contracts with new types of providers.

Debate on the introduction of an own risk system in social health insurance is fierce at the moment. The amount of contributions is to be reconsidered, which will make people more cost conscious and give them joint financial responsibility. (Such responsibility will also result from the introduction of flat rate premiums for social health insurance.)

Social health insurance funds are undergoing a change in their financial system: they are now being budgeted. If the institutions are short of money they can raise their own flat rate premiums. This promotes competition.

The government is also taking some actions towards medical professionals. It is making changes in tariff systems introducing more flexibility and subscription fees, changing transaction fees, giving more value to activities involving contact with patients rather than diagnostic actions. The development of protocols and standards is being promoted by the government. An active scientific general practitioners' society is developing many standards for general practice, and scientific boards of specialists are also speeding up their activities in their field.

The increase of quality, together with the increase of efficiency, is one of the top issues on the government's agenda. Several legislative systems aim at establishing higher quality standards, both for the individual professional and institutions.

A hospital planning act already exists by which it is possible to regulate and centralise specialist care. The government intends to intensify this policy by centralising such care in certain hospitals, mostly university hospitals, by a licensing system.

Finally, the government is making a great effort to strengthen the position of the individual patient as well as patients' organisations. This of course is a very difficult process. Proposals have been submitted to parliament for, among other things, patient–doctor relations, a new complaint system, and revision of the disciplinary system. It is hard to know what the effect will be. The basic question is whether a critical, well informed patient is going to ask for more or for less care.

---

1 *Choices in health care: a report by the government committee on choices in health care.* Rijswijk, Netherlands: Ministry of Health, Welfare and Cultural Affairs, 1992. (AJ Dunning, chairman.)

6 Priority setting in the NHS: reports from six districts

CHRIS HAM

The establishment of district health authorities as purchasers of health services for their residents is a key element in the NHS reforms. In their role as purchasers, district health authorities are responsible for assessing the population's need for health care and deciding which services to buy to meet this need. Operating within cash limited budgets determined by regional health authorities, district health authorities have to agree priorities for the use of the resources they have at their disposal. In part these priorities are intended to reflect policies laid down by ministers and regional health authorities, and in part they are meant to be a response to the assessment of needs carried out locally by district health authorities. Given that not everything can be done within the available resources, district health authorities are therefore in the position of making choices on the use of their funds and the priorities that should be pursued.

This responsibility is not new to district health authorities, who have long been in the position of having to determine local priorities for service development. What is different is that, as purchasers, district health authorities may be able to take decisions which depend less on the demands of providers than they have in the past. In so doing, district health authorities should be able to place greater weight on other factors, such as the views of local people and evidence on the cost effectiveness of different services.

In simplified form, figure 1 shows the situation in which district health authorities find themselves. If, in the past, factors along the vertical axis, represented by national and regional "givens" and

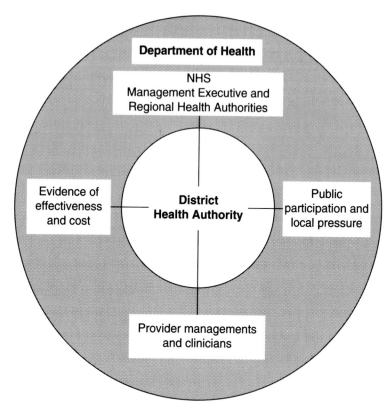

FIG 1—District health authorities find themselves caught between rational and regional "givens" and demands of local professional interests (vertical axis) and public views and research evidence (horizontal axis).[1]

the demands of local professional interests, have been particularly influential, in the future there is an opportunity to attach greater emphasis to public views and research evidence. To underscore the importance of the horizontal axis, experience in Oregon suggests that it was precisely this combination of public opinion and analysis of data drawn from the scientific literature that influenced the decisions of the Health Services Commission, set up to determine priorities for the use of Medicaid funds.

How have district health authorities responded to the challenge of priority setting? A recent study of six authorities who were known to have taken a particular interest in priority setting contains some early indications of likely developments. The study reviewed experience in City and Hackney, Mid Essex, Oxfordshire, Solihull, Southampton and South West Hampshire, and Wandsworth district health authorities up to December 1992. Interviews were conducted with those most closely involved in priority setting, and relevant papers and reports were analysed. The aim was to describe the approach taken in each district, evaluate the lessons that had emerged, and identify implications for the future. The rest of this paper summarises the results of the study, and the full report will be available shortly.[2]

Findings from six districts

The district health authorities in the study had on the whole avoided excluding services entirely from their contracts. This is important because much of the public debate about priority setting has centred on districts where services like tattoo removal and in vitro fertilisation are no longer funded by health authorities. In place of exclusions, there was growing interest in the development of guidelines on which patients are most likely to benefit from particular treatments. This is discussed further below.

A second finding was that district health authorities experienced difficulty in comparing quite different services. This is because there is no common currency for making these broad comparisons. Weighing the priority that should be given to health promotion as against additional operations to reduce waiting times for surgery or higher quality of care for people with learning difficulties is like comparing apples, oranges, and kiwi fruit. At present, there is no reliable basis on which to make these judgments, although over time the development of league tables for cost per QALY (quality adjusted life year) may provide an aid to decision making. In this study, there was very little evidence that the research on QALYs had exerted any influence on district health authorities. Indeed, there seems to be a considerable gap between the work of health economists in this area and the world in which purchasers operate.

Linked to this, a third issue is that district health authorities were able to make more progress by analysing priorities within individual service areas or disease categories than by comparing different services. One example of this was found in Oxfordshire, where the authority was seeking to examine the scope for redistributing resources within the existing envelope of expenditure allocated to individual service areas so that it could obtain additional

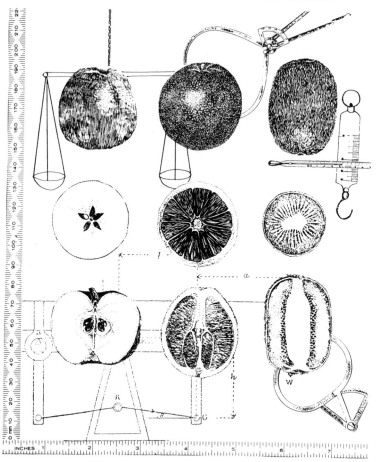

FIG 2—Comparing different services—health promotion as against additional operations to reduce waiting times for surgery or higher quality of care for people with learning difficulties—is like comparing apples, oranges, and kiwi fruit.

health gain. For example, in the case of heart disease, it was considering spending less on inpatient admission for myocardial infarction and more on coronary rehabilitation.

Another example was the approach taken in Wandsworth to review the use of resources for the prevention and treatment of diabetes. In this case, a health economist employed by the health authority had shown how a large volume of resources was spent on a small number of patients. These patients had multiple health and social problems and were admitted to hospital for lengthy stays.

Much less money was spent on a large number of patients looked after by general practitioners and diabetologists. This type of analysis, involving the examination of priorities in terms of "bite-sized chunks," showed the potential for using resources more effectively within individual disease categories.

A fourth finding, and one that is particularly significant, is that the absence of information to guide priority setting was perceived as a major problem everywhere. In particular, information on the cost effectiveness of services was often lacking or incomplete. The effectiveness bulletins put out by the universities of Leeds and York had started to fill some of the gaps that exist and were welcomed by those involved in purchasing.[3] But there was a view that much more could be done to summarise the results of research on the effectiveness of different interventions and to present this in a form that could be readily assimilated by busy managers and their colleagues.

Fifthly, a major effort had been made to involve the public in decision making. One of the reasons for this is the district health authorities recognise that priority setting cannot be reduced to a technical or scientific exercise. Inevitably, the process of setting priorities involves making judgments on the basis of incomplete information and evidence. These judgments are likely to be more soundly based and defensible if they have been exposed to public discussion. In other words, given that there is no right answer in the priority setting debate, an important justification for the decisions that are made is that they have been arrived at as a result of due process.

A variety of methods has been used to involve the public in decision making. For example, in Solihull the district health authority has undertaken a survey of public attitudes to elicit views on the value of different health states and on priorities for service development. This was done through a questionnaire survey of 600 adults.

City and Hackney District Health Authority has also sought the public's views through a questionnaire survey. This was supplemented by meetings with community groups, at which 350 people were interviewed, and by open public meetings. The public's rankings of 16 services was compared with the priorities expressed by general practitioners, consultants, and public health doctors. As the table shows, the public's views in some cases were appreciably different from those of the medical respondents.

Main results of a public priorities survey in City and Hackney Health Authority, 1992. Values are mean priority ranks (1 = highest priority, 16 = lowest)

Services or treatments (examples)	Public (n = 335)	General practitioners (n = 66)	Consultants (n = 116)	Public health doctors (n = 6)*
Treatments for children with life threatening illness (leukaemia)	1	5	2	9
Special care and pain relief for people who are dying (hospice care)	2	4	4	8
Medical research for new treatments	3	11	8	11
High technology surgery and procedures which treat life threatening conditions (heart or liver transplants)	4	12	12	12
Preventive services (screening, immunisation)	5	6	7	4
Surgery to help people with disabilities to carry out everyday tasks (hip replacements)	6	8	5	5 (equal)
Therapy to help people with disabilities carry out everyday tasks (speech therapy, physiotherapy, occupational therapy)	7	7	10	5 (equal)
Services for people with mental illness (psychiatric wards, community psychiatric nurses)	8	2	1	1 (equal)
Intensive care for premature babies who weigh less than one and a half pounds and are unlikely to survive	9	13	13	15 (equal)
Long stay care (hospital and nursing home for elderly people)	10	3	6	10
Community services or care at home (district nurses)	11	1	3	1 (equal)
Health education services (campaigns encouraging healthy lifestyles)	12	10	11	5 (equal)
Family planning services (contraception)	13	9	9	1 (equal)
Treatments for infertility (test tube babies)	14	14	14	15 (equal)
Complementary or alternative medicine (acupuncture, homoeopathy, herbalism)	15	15	16	13 (equal)
Cosmetic surgery (tatto removal, removal of disfiguring lumps and bumps)	16	16	15	13 (equal)

* Little can be construed from this sample as numbers were very small.
Source: Bowling, Jacobson, and Southgate.[7]

Another important finding from the City and Hackney project was that the public's assessment of priorities depended critically on the wording of the questions put to them. As an example, intensive care for premature babies was ranked highly when the survey questionnaire was piloted. Subsequently, when the question was qualified with the statement "babies weighing less than one and a half pounds and are unlikely to survive," its ranking dropped considerably. This has important implications for the design of questionnaires and the methods used to understand the public's views.

A different approach to public participation has been pursued in Mid Essex Health Authority. A number of methods have been used in Mid Essex, including collaboration with the community health council, working with voluntary organisations to discuss and rank priorities for service developments, and making use of the rapid appraisal technique in one part of the district to gather data about the community's views and values. Information from these different sources has been used by the health authority to determine how to allocate its growth funds. In 1992, this consisted of giving particular priority to mental health services.

Tools for priority setting

A sixth finding was that a wide range of tools and methods have been developed to support work on priority setting. Again, Mid Essex exemplifies this, having used a variety of tools to identify priorities. These include a device known as 16 health care building blocks, a list of priorities originally developed by the BBC's Public Eye documentary programme, and a similar exercise prepared in the district which has been used to rank 12 services in order of priority. The purpose of all of these tools is to explore with a variety of interests (general practitioners, community health councils, voluntary organisations, etc) the relative priority attached to different services.

In City and Hackney, as well as research to investigate how the public viewed priorities, the director of public health has developed a two stage scoring method to help inform priority setting. In the first stage, bids are ranked on the basis of needs assessment, with greatest weight being attached to services which respond to local needs. In the second stage, after a shortlist has been prepared, individual proposals are ranked by using the following criteria:

- Robustness or implementability of proposal (scored 0–3)
- Promotion of equity (0–1)
- Evidence of effectiveness or cost effectiveness (0–2)
- Collaboration with or integration with primary care (0–3)
- Prioritised by community health council (0–1)
- Prioritised by general practitioners or general practitioners' forum (0–1)

- Other possible or more appropriate sources of funding (0–5; negative score).

The greatest weight is therefore attached to whether other funding methods are available, using a negative score as high as five to cancel out the other weightings.

A similar method is used in Wandsworth. In 1992–3, proposals were ranked by using the following criteria and weightings up to a possible score of 100:

- Gives potential for health gain (40)
- Improves quality of service (20)
- Accords with local views (20)
- Achievable in current year (15)
- Accords with national and regional priorities (5).

In this approach, potential for health gain is an all embracing factor encompassing length of life as well as quality. The ranking exercise was undertaken among both the purchasing team and the non-executive members of the district health authority, and an agreed list of priorities was drawn up at the end of the exercise.

Impact

One of the questions that inevitably arises from the work done so far is, what impact has it had on decision making? In some districts, of which Solihull is probably the best example, the answer is that there has so far been a very limited impact. This is largely because the work carried out in Solihull was still being analysed at the time when the research was done and it would be premature to expect major changes to have occurred.

In other districts, and here Mid Essex is a good example, it is possible to point to decisions that have been shaped by the interest shown in priority setting. The decisions to give higher priority to mental health services was a direct reflection of the discussions that took place locally with key interests. Similarly, in City and Hackney the district health authority decided to protect community services in the face of considerable pressure to allocate extra resources to acute services.

In the remaining districts, the impact of the work done has been real but less tangible. Managers in these districts refer to a change in the culture of their organisations and a new approach to thinking about priorities without being able to cite specific examples of decisions that have been altered. No doubt this is partly because of the interest shown in exercises and simulations of priority setting in districts like Oxfordshire, Southampton and South West Hampshire, and Wandsworth. It is also because some of the analysis has been research based and was not designed with the aim of directly influencing purchasing decisions at this stage.

Despite this it is possible to show that the investment of time and effort has made a difference. Examples include Oxfordshire, where agreement has been reached on the values that shape purchasing, and Southampton and South West Hampshire, where the emphasis placed on widespread consultation on priorities illustrates how the process of purchasing has been influenced. This in turn has helped to frame the strategic priorities set out in the purchasing plan. Similarly, in Wandsworth the development of criteria for ranking bids for development has made more explicit the basis on which decisions are reached.

Emerging issues

The conclusion to emerge from this study is that district health authorities are still at an early stage in the development of their work on priority setting. The six districts whose work has been studied were chosen because they were known to be particularly interested in the process of priority setting. As such, they could make some claim to being at the leading edge of development in this particular area. Despite this it is clear that only limited progress has been made to date.

It is also apparent that a good deal of innovation is occurring in these districts. In the absence of a national strategy on the part of the government to set priorities for the NHS as a whole, district health authorities have taken the lead in developing approaches which they believe are appropriate. This makes it difficult to generalise about the work that had been done so far because a wide range of initiatives has been launched. As further experience is gained it will be important to find a way of sharing local knowledge to enable other health authorities to learn from the work that has been done.

On the basis of this study it is apparent that district health authorities could be assisted in the work they are doing if there were a more concerted approach nationally to draw together information on effectiveness and cost effectiveness in a usable form. Although the effectiveness bulletins produced by the universities of Leeds and York are seen as useful, it is not clear why the topics they cover have been chosen (glue ear and screening for osteoporosis are hardly at the top of the NHS agenda) and it would help purchasers if cost effectiveness data were available in relation to services which are clearly at the centre of government policy. Nowhere is this more important than in relation to *The Health of the Nation*. District health authorities have no choice but to pursue the objectives set out in the national health strategy, but they do have discretion in selecting the means for their achievement. At its simplest, this means identifying the comparative costs and benefits of the preventive and treatment strategies that might be adopted in working towards the government's targets for coronary heart disease, cancer, and other priority areas.

Much the same applies in relation to the shift from secondary to primary care. District health authorities are showing increasing interest in this issue as they work more closely with general practitioners. What is lacking at present is information and evidence that summarises views on best practice to enable district health authorities to decide which kind of services can be provided most appropriately and effectively in and around a primary care setting. This includes not only issues such as the treatment of asthma and diabetes but also the role of specialists in doing some of their outpatient work alongside general pratitioners, the scope for extending minor surgery and investigations in primary care, and the use of staff such as physiotherapists, dietitians, and counsellors in general practice. There was a strong feeling among those interviewed that much of this information is available but it has yet to percolate through to those responsible for developing purchasing plans.

One approach worth examining is the work done in Wales to produce protocols for investment in health gain. The stated purpose of these protocols is to discern areas where further investment would bring worthwhile health gain. Topics covered include cancer, cardiovascular disease, maternal and early child health and physical and sensory disabilities. Drawing on research findings and expert views, each protocol provides an assessment of need and identifies options for meeting this need through changes in priorities or service delivery. As such, published reports provide a resource for use by health authorities. While elements of this approach exist in England (for example, the needs assessment work commissioned by the NHS Management Executive) there is no comparable work which brings together information on needs and service effectiveness in a form that is accessible to health authorities.

In this context, the research undertaken by James Raftery seems to offer a way forward. This research combines a disease MAPping approach with evidence on cost effectiveness. Disease MAPs—measurements of activity and price—provide information on the numbers of people suffering from particular diseases and on associated patterns of expenditure. Drawing on available data on cost effectiveness and making use of comparative health service indicators, Raftery has matched the use of health service facilities to the resources consumed. This approach (unpublished data) can be applied to support work on priority setting for health gain.

Future developments

In emphasising the need to provide better information to support work on priority setting, the importance of other inputs to decision making should not be neglected. Above all, further work is needed to establish the most appropriate ways of involving the public in decision making. The experience of City and Hackney Health Authority serves as a cautionary tale. The way in which questions are framed seems to influence the responses that are given. Any attempt to seek the public's views needs to incorporate this lesson. Indeed, given the complexity of some of the choices that have to be made, it may be that an investment in informing and educating the public about the issues involved is needed before citizens are asked to list priorities in rank order.

To return to an earlier point, one particularly promising path for further development is the use of guidelines to identify those patients who are most likely to benefit from particular interventions. The value of guidelines has been acknowledged by a committee set up by the Dutch government to examine choices in health care. The Dunning committee argued that guidelines should be drawn up by professional and scientific bodies as one part of a strategy for approaching priority setting.[4] In particular, guidelines were seen to be important in ensuring the appropriate use of services.

In this context, appropriateness refers both to the selection of patients (restricting treatment to those patients who can clearly

69

benefit) and to the care setting (home care; primary care; out-patient, day patient, and inpatient care). The underlying argument here is that a focus on appropriateness should enable better use to be made of available resources. This is a central thrust of the approach adopted by general practitioner fundholders, who maintain that they are achieving significant improvements in services through delivering these services more appropriately. The existence of wide variations in clinical practices[5] suggests that there is considerable scope for change in this respect.

An unanswered question is whether the greater use of guidelines will obviate the need to define more precisely the boundaries of NHS provision. More specifically, would it be necessary to exclude a wider range of services from the NHS? At the time of writing there are conflicting indications on this point. On the one hand, it would seem that some services, such as long term nursing care, are increasingly being excluded in many places, and others (dental care for adults, for example) may be added. On the other hand, there is the experience of New Zealand, where a committee set up by the government in 1992 to identify core services to be available in the public health scheme concluded that this was not best done by drawing up a list of such services. As the committee noted, the starting point of any analysis should be that existing services reflected "decades of reasonably commonsense and principled decision making."[6] As such, these services could be said to constitute the core of service provision.

Like the Dunning committee, the New Zealand core services committee went on to argue that greater attention should be paid to the appropriate use of all services. To assist in this process it initiated a series of consensus conferences to develop guidelines for using specific interventions. As the debate about priority setting develops in the United Kingdom, it is this focus on what were earlier referred to as bite sized chunks of service provision that seems to hold out most promise.

This paper is based on research carried out in association with Frank Honigsbaum and David Thompson. I thank them for their assistance. Thanks are also due to the Research and Development Directorate in the NHS Management Executive, which supported this research.

1 Heginbotham C, Ham C. *Purchasing dilemmas*. London: King's Fund College, 1992.
2 Ham C, Honigsbaum F, Thompson D. *Priority setting for health gain*. London: NHS Management Executive (in press).
3 University of Leeds; University of York. *Effective health care*. Leeds. The Universities, 1992, 1993.

4 Ministry of Welfare, Health, and Cultural Affairs. *Choices in health care.* Rijswijk: The Ministry, 1992. (Dunning report.)
5 Ham C, ed. *Health care variations.* London: King's Fund Institute, 1988.
6 National Advisory Committee. *Core services 1993/4.* Wellington: NAC, 1992.
7 Bowling A, Jacobson B, Southgate L. Health service priorities: explorations in consultation of the public and health professionals on priority setting in an inner London health district. *Soc Sci Med* 1993;**37**:851–7.

PART III: THE THEORY

7 Economics of priority setting: let's ration rationally!

CAM DONALDSON

Economics and priority setting go hand in hand. They are both based on the undeniable fact that resources are scarce. If this statement is taken as given, no dilemma should be involved in accepting that choices then have to be made about what services to purchase and what not to purchase (or provide, depending on how one looks at it). That is, priorities have to be set. Economists have been peddling these basic premises of scarcity and choice for many years,[1] and so has the NHS—it is just that no one seemed to notice until recently. Choices have often been made implicitly, and older and more recent policy documents have given very little guidance on how to go about priority setting.[2-5]

Much of the recent debate about choice in the NHS has focused on the term "rationing."[6] It seems that writers who use this more emotive expression for choice have a higher probability of catching and maintaining people's imaginations. Therefore, the term "rationing" will be used in lieu of "choice" for the remainder of this paper. As with choice, there should be no dilemma in accepting that rationing exists. It happens, and the only dilemma is in deciding how to ration. How should priorities be set?

For an economist considering this question the first port of call is the market. I will discuss why rationing is not left to less regulated market forces, and in the main section of the paper I will outline alternatives for rationing within a more regulated system, one in which almost all health care is publicly financed and provided. If the aim of health services is to maximise benefits to the community (subject to resource and equity constraints) then the economic approach to rationing is the one that should be adopted.

Leave it to the market?

The type of market referred to in this section is a less regulated market, not the highly regulated health care market that is now in place in the United Kingdom. It is important to consider less regulated markets for two reasons. Firstly, the bottom line is that if governments decided not to finance or provide health care, a market for such care would always arise. Secondly, at intervals an unregulated market for health care is proposed.[78] It is important, therefore, to discuss why such markets do not work well for health care.

Why not leave it to the market and ration by price? This has one great advantage—no waiting lists! Any possible excess demand on the system is choked off by the pricing mechanism before people reach the service. Of course, waiting time might be viewed as a characteristic of the service. Individuals might choose to buy services with more or less of this characteristic. However, in such an environment, in which individuals are "free" to choose their waiting time, waiting lists would not be as controversial and politicised as they are in the NHS now.

But such market systems have fatal flaws (figure).[9] The first is that markets tend to work well for goods about which consumers are fairly well informed as to their preferences and when the need for the good will arise. This may be the case for foodstuffs but it is not so for health care.

In an unregulated environment the market response to such uncertainty would be the development of health care insurance markets. In such markets it is likely that excessive demands for care will result. Once the premium is paid, consumers will have no incentive to moderate their demands. A third party, the insurance company, pays for care. Likewise, doctors will have no incentive to moderate care to meet such demands. Not only does a third party pay but also that third party does not put an overall spending cap on the system. Often in such systems, costs, in terms of increasing premiums, are passed on to a fourth party. Fourth parties are employers who pay or subsidise their employees' premiums. Witness the problems in the United States, where about one eighth of the nation's resources are now spent on health care.[10]

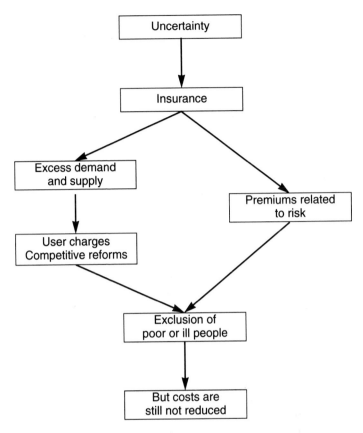

Flaws of unregulated health care markets

A possible mechanism for controlling such "excessive" demands is user charges, whereby patients are required to pay a proportion (up to a maximum amount) of their medical bill out of their own pockets. In addition, in such systems insurance premiums tend to be related to people's risks of using services. These lead to the second flaw of such systems. Given the association between poverty and ill health, the very people who will be most liable to pay charges and higher insurance premiums will be those most in need of care. A proportion of such people with lower incomes will not be able to afford charges or insurance. They experience problems with access to care. It has already been agreed that such lack of access among certain sections of society is largely unacceptable in the health care systems of developed nations, except perhaps in the United States.

One reason why problems of access among less well off people may not worry all doctors in the United States is because doctors have the power to induce demand for health care.[11] Thus demand can be induced for care for those able and willing to pay. This maintains doctors' incomes. The system chugs along at the same, or even an increasing, level of activity. But less benefit is produced, because the induced care generally produces less benefit than if it had been directed at less well off groups.

One way round this, within a less regulated system, is to introduce publicly funded mechanisms to ensure access, such as the Medicare and Medicaid schemes in the United States. Thus, even in what has been referred to as "the rhetorically 'free enterprise' USA,"[12] 41% of health care expenditure in 1984 was publicly financed. But inevitably people fall between the cracks.[13] Recently it was estimated that 37 million people in the United States (17% of the population) had no cover (public or private) whatsoever.[14]

In addition, such mechanisms usually end up being cumbersome and expensive. The same is true of competitive reforms, managed care, and utilisation review, all introduced with the aim of making American health care more efficient. The effect of such activities has been described: "A large and growing share of the American total is spent, not on doctors and nurses, but on accountants, management consultants and public realtions specialists. Their contribution to the health of the American population is difficult to discern (unless one is trained in neoclassical economics and is able to see with the eye of faith)."[12]

A recent published estimate put the cost of administration and management of the American health care system at 22% of total health care costs.[15] Many would see that as a characterisation of the current waiting list problem in the United Kingdom. In a cash limited system, when more managers are employed to run the new NHS market, something has to give. Elective surgery is an obvious target. Hence the waiting list problem. But that is another story.

The upshot is that we have health care systems (or markets) which, for the most part, involve public finance and provision. The market for health care in Britain is no exception. It is very highly regulated. But that in itself does not solve our rationing problem.

How should priorities be set in highly regulated health care markets?

Rationing in public systems

There are four alternatives for rationing within public systems. The first three will be covered only briefly.

Ostrich economics

The first alternative is to have no explicit rationing. Society seems comfortable with this. It perpetuates the pretence that there is no rationing at all. But it does not permit any definition of objectives and, more importantly for the research community, it does not allow analysis of whether such objectives are being met.

It is romantic.[16] It fails to recognise the first premise of economics, scarcity of resources, because it denies the inevitability of choice. This approach is impotent to deal with the basic problems that face every society. Unfortunately, there are times when romance is unhelpful and this is one of them.

A realistic argument against explicit rationing is that the techniques, such as QALYs (quality adjusted life years), on which it might be based are imperfect.[17] Such limitations are recognised by some proponents of more explicit rationing.[18] It is now a well worn phrase of economists that economics is an *aid* to decision making and not the sole decision making tool.

Burden of illness

The rationale behind the burden of illness approach is that priority, either in terms of health care resources or researchers' time, should go to alleviating or analysing diseases which are the big killers or big spenders in society. Heart disease is the most obvious case. This approach is essentially the one that was taken in *The Health of the Nation*[3] and underlies much activity in needs assessment for purchasing services in the new NHS.[19]

There are two problems with such an approach. Firstly, it provides no rules for resource allocation. How many resources should be devoted to treatment and prevention of heart disease relative to other diseases? Arbitrary rules can be drawn up, such as

Box 1—(Mis)interpreting waiting lists		
	Good care	Bad care
Long list	Care is good, so GPs refer more	Use of outmoded care (five-day stays)
Short list	Use of effective day care	Care is bad, so GPs refer less

allocating resources to diseases pro rata according to the size of the problem.

Secondly, such arbitrary rules are unlikely to result in maximisation of benefits to the community from available resources. This is because the approach ignores the cost and productivity of treatment and prevention. A treatment like chiropody seems to come out well in terms of health gain produced for resources spent, yet foot problems are unlikely to get any attention under the burden of illness approach.[20]

Indicative rationing

The third approach is to ration according to indicators, such as waiting lists. Not much research has been carried out on the interpretation and meaning of waiting lists, so it is difficult to interpret current data. A very simple and naive example is given in box 1. The explanation for a long waiting time can be that quality of care is good. General practitioners may perceive this to be the case and refer more people. Alternatively, a long waiting time can result because outmoded care (say five day stay instead of same day for appropriate elective surgery) is being practised. Likewise with short waiting times. Thus, long or short waiting times can occur for good or bad reasons. Another problem with regard to waiting lists is that they are largely indicators of what people do *not* do rather than what they *do* do.

Other indicators are measures of activity, such as numbers of patients treated. These measure what people do, but not the "success" of such activity. Is it necessary to treat more patients? If so, are the right groups being treated? The only way to answer such questions is to have data on the outcomes of such activities.

The economic rationale for rationing

This leads to the fourth approach, which is the one I advocate. At this stage economists politely suggest to their readers that they should employ a rational economic approach, allocating resources according to principles of equity and efficiency. When, on one hand, groups are calling for more resources for health care, while on the other hand groups are telling the service to be more efficient, and neither produce any decent evidence either way, it is difficult to come to any other conclusion.

The theoretical basis of the rational economic approach is the principle of opportunity cost. Earlier, it was stated that scarcity leads to a need to choose what to purchase and what not to purchase (that is, rationing). This means that certain opportunities will be foregone. Economists refer to the benefits associated with these foregone opportunities as opportunity costs. The aim is to maximise benefits and, conversely, minimise opportunity cost. This is an efficiency objective.

As a brief aside, economists are also concerned with equity. Indeed economists are some of the most prolific writers on the subject.[21][22] However, equity principles are difficult to agree on and to measure. What we can be sure of, though, is that their implementation will still result in some groups being excluded from receiving care. This is because the need for equity principles is also based on scarcity. If there were enough resouces for everyone to have what they need or want, we would not have to decide on which groups in society get what.

The implications of efficiency principles are easier to agree on. They are that, first, we need to measure the costs and benefits of health care. If the aim is to maximise benefits, the only way to do this is to measure costs and benefits and choose the combination of health care that maximises benefits for available resources. This sounds like a daunting task, the economist's dream of measuring costs and benefits of everything. Fortunately, it is not necessary, due to another trick of economics: the margin (box 2).

The margin is concerned with change. Starting with a given mix of services, what are important are the costs and benefits of changes from that given mix. If the mix of services can be changed to produce greater benefit, then this should be done. The costs and benefits of changes are marginal costs and benefits. The implication of this is that we do not have to measure the costs and benefits

---

Box 2—The margin

- The margin is concerned with change (and not necessarily small changes)
- Start with a given mix of services
- What are important are the costs and benefits of changes from that given mix
- If the mix of services can be reorientated to produce more benefit, this should be done

---

Box 3—Getting started with priority setting[18]

- Define programmes
- Establish programme management groups
- Draw up candidates for expansion and contraction
- Analyse costs and benefits in whatever terms are possible
- Choose

---

of every existing service, only costs and benefits of proposed changes in services.

Getting started

So much for the principles. Even marginal analysis seems a bit daunting. Where do you start? Moving towards the more practical end of the spectrum, it is possible at least to provide a first stab at an answer to that question.

The first point listed in box 3 is to start within programmes, rather than attempt to compare disparate alternatives. This gives some chance of getting homogeneity of outputs across interventions to be considered. The group responsible for priority setting for each programme should draw up a list of candidates for service reduction and expansion. These are the margins whose costs and benefits will be looked at in more detail. Candidates for reduction will be those about which there is doubt about benefit achieved for resources spent. Candidates for expansion can also include new services. Then fairly standard steps would be followed to assess costs and benefits.[18 23] According to principles of efficiency, the candidates which are chosen for retention, introduction, or expansion will be those offering greater benefits per pound spent.

Conclusion

The implementation of the economic approach in the new NHS is not easy. One caveat is that we need to know how to define and measure benefit. Health gain is probably the most important element. But other aspects like autonomy (of patients, not doctors) and the process of care are particularly important for some groups. At this stage benefit should be measured in whatever terms are possible. Better to have rough and ready (but improving) estimates of the right things than accurate measures of the wrong things.

The economic approach is about maximisation of benefit to the community per pound spent. This is a laudable objective based on two simple principles, opportunity cost and marginal analysis. If the setting of the health care budget is not to be left in the hands of those providing unsubstantiated arguments in favour of expansion or cuts then the future of health care priority and budget setting must, to a degree, rest with the application of these principles.

The Health Economics Research Unit is funded by the Chief Scientist Office of the Scottish Office Home and Health Department. The opionions expressed in this paper are those of the author, not the department.

1 Williams A. The cost-benefit approach. *Br Med Bull*, 1974; **30**: 252–6.
2 Department of Health and Social Security. *Priorities for health and personal social services in England*. London: HMSO, 1976.
3 Secretary of State for Health. *The health of the nation*. London: HMSO, 1992.
4 NHS Management Executive. *Moving forward—needs, services and contracts*. London: NHS Management Executive, March 1991. (DHA project paper.)
5 NHS Management Executive. *Assessing health care needs*. London: NHS Management Executive, May 1991. (DHA project discussion paper.)
6 Smith R. Rationing: the search for sunlight. *BMJ* 1991; **303**: 1651–2.
7 Green D. *Which doctor?* London: Institute of Economic Affairs, 1986.
8 Logan J, Green D, Woodfield A. *Healthy competition*. Sydney: Centre for Independent studies, 1989.
9 Donaldson C, Gerard K. *Economics of health care financing: the visible hand*. London: Macmillan, 1993.
10 Organisation for Economic Cooperation and Development. *Financing and delivering health care: a comparative analysis of OECD countries*. Paris: OECD, 1987. (Social policy studies No 4.)
11 Krasnick A, Groenewegen PP, Pederson PA, Scholten P, Mooney G, Gottschau A, *et al.* Changing remuneration systems: effects on activity in general practice. *BMJ* 1990; **300**: 1698–701.
12 Evans RG. Tension, compression and shear: directions, stresses and outcomes of health care cost control. *J Health Polit Policy Law* 1990; 15: 101–28.
13 Donaldson C, Mooney G. The new NHS in a global context: is it taking us where we want to be? *Health Policy* (in press).
14 Wilensky GR. Filling the gaps in health insurance. *Health Affairs* 1988; 7: 133–49.

15 Woolhandler S, Himmelstein DU. The deteriorating administrative efficiency of the US health care system. *N Engl J Med* 1991; **324**: 1253–8.
16 Mooney G. *Economics, medicine and health care*. 2nd ed. Brighton: Wheatshealf, 1992.
17 Hunter D. *Rationing dilemmas in health care*. Birmingham: National Association of Health Authorities and Trusts, 1992. (Research paper No 8.)
18 Mooney G, Gerard K, Donaldson C, Farrar S. *Priority setting in purchasing: some practical guidelines*. Birmingham: National Association of Health Authorities and Trusts, 1992. (Research paper No 6.)
19 Donaldson C, Mooney G. Needs assessment, priority setting and contracts for health care: an economic view. *BMJ* 1991; **303**: 1529–30.
20 Bryan S, Parkin D, Donaldson C. Chiropody and the QALY: a case study in assigning categories of disability and distress to patients. *Health Policy* 1991; **18**: 169–85.
21 Wagstaff A, van Doorslaer E, Paci P. On the measurement of horizontal equity in the delivery of health care. *J Health Econ* 1991; **10**: 169–205.
22 Mooney G, Hall J, Donaldson C, Gerard K. Utilisation as a measure of equity: weighing heat? *J Health Econ* 1991; **10**: 475–80.
23 Donaldson C, Farrar S. Needs assessment: developing an economic approach. *Health Policy* (in press).

8 Justice in priority setting

RUTH CHADWICK

It is now widely accepted that we cannot "do everything" in health care: we have to set priorities. We cannot be said to have obligations, as a society, to do what we cannot, for as Kant pointed out, ought implies can.[1] There is no excuse or justification, however, for doing less than we can. Although it is true that health is only one social good, it remains the case that among social goods health has a special status, as people's health radically affects their ability to enjoy other social goods. In turn, social conditions such as unemployment affect people's chances of enjoying good health— this is why it is appropriate to call health a social rather than a natural good. This is in contrast to the Rawlsian position, which classified health as a natural good, failing adequately to take into account the interaction between social justice and health status.[2] The first way in which justice impinges on the priority setting debate, then, is in the impact of social justice generally on health. This suggests that one priority may be to identify ways of improving health that are distinct from provision of health care.

It might be argued that in the specific context of priority setting in the health service the concept to turn to is efficiency rather than justice. It seems clear, however, that while efficiency is desirable it is also important to have a method of priority setting that is fair. In this paper I do not claim to be offering a solution to the question of what is fair. Daniels is right, I think, to say that much more groundwork needs to be done on theories of justice before they can hope to give definitive answers in this context.[3] What I aim to do is to elucidate some of the issues. A preliminary point is that

85

considerations of justice are relevant at both macro and micro levels of priority setting.

Of the theoretical perspectives on priority setting, justice is among the most difficult. Justice is known as an "essentially contested" concept—that is, there are competing conceptions of justice, all of which have respectable arguments in their favour.[4] I shall consider three. It is possible, however, to give a general account of the concept, with regard to which the competing conceptions compete, and this was done by Aristotle in the following way: "Justice consists in treating equals equally and unequals unequally, in proportion to their relevant differences."

This may seem impossibly abstract, but in fact it is a remarkably powerful statement. The point is that there is a presumption in favour of equality, which can justly be departed from only in cases where there is a difference relevant to the treatment in question. It is a statement such as this that is behind our by now well established opposition to discrimination on the grounds of race, sex, and sexual orientation. Debate over the relevance of age, however, as a difference relevant to health care allocation continues (see, for example, Hunt and Callahan[5]).

Aristotle's definition naturally leads us to assume that people have an equal right to health care, unless some relevant difference can be found to justify giving priority to some over others. (We must not delude ourselves that in giving priority to treatments or specialisms rather than people we are not actually affecting people, because of course we are.)

The statement quoted from Aristotle, however, does not give us any clues as to what counts as a relevant difference. For this reason it is known as a formal definition of justice. It is with regard to the nature of the relevant differences that the competing conceptions differ most clearly. They also, however, take different positions on the sense in which people are said to be equal. The three conceptions are desert, need, and utility.

Desert

It is sometimes said that the idea that people should get their just deserts is one of the deepest and most tenacious intuitions about justice.[6] Desert is the relevant difference to consider. The idea is common (though not uncontroversial) in thinking about criminal justice, but whether it is appropriate in the health care setting is

Aspects of justice and desert
Lifestyle and just deserts
Equality of opportunity
Individual as free chooser
Individual responsibility

problematic. One side of it is the view that a person's or a group's lifestyle may be relevant to whether or not they "deserve" priority in health care—for example, do they smoke or indulge in unsafe sex or intravenous drug use? If so, then perhaps they are to blame for their own health status and not deserving of priority.

This view is not appropriate for use in priority setting. Firstly, the language of praise and blame does not carry over well from the context of punishment and reward. Secondly, there is a problem of where to draw the line. Arguably, we all take risks with our health—the use of the motor car, for example, is one of the worst. It might be objected that there is no comparison between drug abuse and driving—that while the former is certain to damage one's health, the latter carries with it a small risk. While this may be the case, the point is that there is no sharp line to be drawn between those who take no risks with their own health and those who do. If we compare smoking and mountain climbing, for example, it becomes clear that there is a difference only in degrees of risk, but social values also play a part in our application of the notion of desert. The Dutch report *Choices in Health Care* has argued, rightly, that it cannot be seen as right to abandon people to their fate on the grounds of disapproval of their lifestyle.[7] There are other aspects to the desert model, however, as it embodies a cluster of related concepts (box).

The punitive aspect of the model described above arises from the view of the individual as a free chooser responsible for the choices made. This again is related to the particular notion of equality embodied in the desert model. People are thought to have equal opportunity to make choices about their own lives. It is showing respect for them as free choosers to evaluate these choices.[6]

These ideas lead to another currently popular idea—individual responsibility for health. The problem with this is that it gives insufficient weight to the social causes of disease and the context in

> **Aspects of justice and need**
> Sense of community
> Treatment as equals
> Definition of need
> Needs:
> - Individual
> - Medical
> - Social
> - Basic needs

which choices are made. As has frequently been pointed out, it may be very difficult in situations of deprivation to make "healthy" choices concerning food and smoking habits. Social justice cannot be exhausted by thinking in terms of individual responsibility. This notion itself has two sides. The Dutch report rightly distinguishes between encouraging individuals to take responsibility for their own health, on the one hand, and depriving them of resources if they do not, on the other.[7] A further distinction has to be made between enabling individuals to take responsibility by providing health education and promotion campaigns (such as on smoking) and making them financially responsible for health when they cannot afford it. The responsibility of the community for those in need cannot be ignored.

Need

The idea of the responsibility of the community takes us towards a competing conception of justice which holds that it is just to allocate resources according to need. Like the desert model, this has some intuitive support—surely a just society would be one that gave individuals what they need? Some go so far as to see it as a logical truth that health care ought to be allocated on the grounds of medical need. Bernard Williams, for example, holds that "the proper ground of distribution of medical care is ill health: this is a necessary truth."[8] Once more we have a set of related ideas in the need model (box).

The need conception is generally considered to be more egalitarian than the desert model. Thus Miller makes the "working assumption" that "egalitarians are committed to the view that justice consists (minimally) in a distribution of resources according to need,"[9] and Raphael suggests that "discrimination in favour of need has an egalitarian purpose."[10] (We should bear in mind, however, that a fully worked through application of desert in social justice generally could have quite radical implications.[11]) The need model is operating with a different understanding of equality. This involves making a distinction between equal treatment and treatment as equals. Obviously it is not the case that equality demands giving everyone equal treatment in the sense of the same prescription, for example—for not everyone needs a given prescription. But people should be treated as equals in the sense that people with equal needs should be given equal consideration, whatever the individual merits of the person.

But who is to say what a person or group needs? Health care needs have been defined in terms of the capacity to benefit from treatment (see, for example, Williams and Frankel[12]). This transfers the problem of defining need to the problem of what counts as benefit, and individuals, health care professionals, and representatives of the community may have different ideas about this. Individuals may feel they have benefited if they receive something they want; health care professionals may determine benefit in terms of restoration to normal functioning; the community may judge the issue by the facilitation of the individual's participation in society.[7]

If we allow individuals or groups to define their own needs we will be subject to the bottomless pit problem. If on the other hand health care professionals determine need, for obvious reasons they are likely to be biased in favour of their own specialisms. If we consult the public about the relative needs of different groups we may be in danger of running into what Daniels calls the democracy problem—the results may be counterintuitive.[3] It is often held, for example, that people who have not suffered from a condition tend to overestimate its severity. This is of particular importance in relation to prenatal genetic counselling with regard to termination of pregnancy. Representatives of groups with a particular condition object to the idea that their lives are held to be so lacking in worth that abortion is thought to be indicated for a fetus diagnosed as affected. However, there is another side to the coin. Some conditions are likely to be systematically underestimated by those who have not suffered from them. An example would be a chronic non-life threatening disease such as severe atopic eczema. The label 'eczema' is used to cover so wide a range of conditions

> ## Problems with the need model
> The bottomless pit problem
> Priorities
> Helping the worst off is inefficient

that to many it signifies a relatively minor skin irritation rather than the pain of whole body inflammation. If, then, the public is consulted about the relative needs of different groups, to what extent is it justifiable to "hand adjust" the outcome, as was done in Oregon?[13]

The difficulties with this question lead to the temptation of defining need by another route. One suggestion is that whether or not it makes sense to say that a group has needs is dependent on whether or not an effective service is available. This is in accordance with the slogan that "ought implies can": it cannot be said that we ought to do what we cannot do, therefore insofar as need is normative it is true to say that it is inappropriate to use the language of need where it is impossible to do anything about it. But need is surely not only normative but also descriptive. It makes sense to say that a person or group is "in need" even if there is as yet no solution. If we deny that the language of need is appropriate where does the moral obligation come from to try to find a solution to the problems of these individuals or groups (for example, a cure for AIDS)? What has to be investigated here, then, is in what sense of "available," if any, it is true to say that no effective service is available.

A further possibility is that we employ a concept of "basic needs." Thus Doyal says, "By basic needs, I mean those preconditions for successful participation within any form of life."[14] Perhaps (if a workable form of public consultation can be developed) need should be determined socially by establishing an agreed standard such as a minimum acceptable level, or the level at which a condition prevents a person or group from participating in society, both contributing to it and gaining from it.

Even if we can solve the definition problem with regard to need, it may still not be possible to satisfy all identified needs because of the "bottomless pit" problem. Then we have to set priorities between needs. Establishing a category of basic needs does not avoid difficulty. If the minimum acceptable level is too low, the

> Aspects of justice and utility
> Medical success
> Concept of utility
> Principle of maximisation
> Each counts for one, and no one for more than one
> The QALY

obligations of the health service to respond to them might seem to be similarly minimalist; on the other hand, if the level is too high, it may not be possible to meet it and priorities would have to be set below it. It might seem "just" to give priority to those whose need is the greatest—to those who are furthest below the minimum acceptable level. There is desire, if not a moral obligation, to relieve the greatest suffering where we can. But this is arguably inefficient. Those who are the worst off might be those who provide the least opportunity for achieving medical success. It is this truth which gives plausibility to the idea that need should be defined in terms of capacity to benefit. (To try to sidestep this problem by talking about "basic care" rather than "basic need" is still problematic[15] and does not enable us to escape the fact that even if we cut services, rather than eligibility, that has the consequence that some people may not get what they need.)

Perhaps we need a concept of medical success to prioritise between needs. It is at this point that the third competing conception of justice comes into the picture: utility.

Utility

According to the utility model, priorities should be set in the light of what is expected to lead to the best possible outcome. Like utilitarianism generally, as a moral theory, the model as applied in the health care context has two elements: a concept of utility and a principle of maximisation (box). In other words, it has a notion of what counts as medical success and also a principle that we ought to aim for as much of it as possible. At first sight, utility might seem to have little to do with justice. Thus Hunter says, "The major flaw in applying utilitarian principles to health care purchasing (and provision) is the lack of justice in such decisions. This justice is encompassed in terms of the inviolability of the individual."[16] Utilitarianism is commonly criticised precisely on the grounds that it legitimates injustice to individuals and minority groups.

There are three points to bear in mind about the relation between utility and justice. The first is that the criticism that utilitarianism is prepared to sacrifice individuals is overstated—in the real world the utilitarian has to bear in mind the disutility of the resentment that would arise from such actions (see, for example, Hare[17]). The second is that, if we are thinking in terms of a just society, if a priority setting policy maximises less utility than it can then fewer people are being helped than could be helped, and surely this is unjust—those who lose out under such an arrangement might understandably see it as unjust. It is not as clear cut as this, however, because much depends on the pattern of distribution of the utility that is gained.

Another way of looking at the relation between utility and justice is in the utility principle itself. It is said to incorporate an idea of justice not in the outcome of maximisation, but in doing the utilitarian calculation, where "each counts for one, and no one for more than one." It is thus associated with an idea of equality—non-discrimination. When the concept of quality adjusted life years was first introduced this idea was incorporated, so that one QALY was said to count for one, no matter whose life it was attached to. Now, however, we hear increasingly about the weighted QALY, which may need to be justified by different criteria of justice (see, for example, Kappel and Sandøe[18]). If, for example, it is argued that a year of healthy life in a mother of three children is worth more than a year of life in a single person, it may be that ideas about desert in terms of social worth are being introduced which are distorting the model.

Problems with the utility model

The distribution problem arises from the fact that the principle of maximising our outcome measure, such as QALYs, does not tell us how to distribute them. Although in general QALYs have sometimes been accused of being agist,[19] we might be able to achieve the same number of QALYs by directing our resources to a small number of young people as to a greater number of elderly people. The QALY measure itself does not tell us which to choose, because it is not primarily interested in people at all. Thus Nord says that a problematic feature of the QALY approach is "its focus

> ## Problems with the utility model
> The distribution problem
> The "persons in need" problem

on quality of life in life years rather than quality of life in people. In health care policy making this is a somewhat strange and artificial perspective. The health services . . . are concerned with providing care for living, breathing, feeling and thinking numbers, not with maximising numbers of abstract time entities."[20]

Nord's work points us to the "persons in need" problem: the feeling remains that we should not follow outcomes to the extent of ignoring the actual suffering of real people. Nord's research on attitudes in Norway has suggested that in that society, at least, it would be inappropriate to introduce a criterion for priority setting that concentrated on outcomes at the expense of a concern for people's need. An empirical study (though based on a small sample) suggested that, faced with choice between different people in the same bad state, respondents valued equality in entitlement to treatment rather than health after treatment.[21]

For some, the notion of entitlement to treatment indicates the desirability of a certain randomness in allocation, either by "first come, first served"[21] or by lottery.[19] Yet it does not seem to be right that the notion that "each counts for one" must be interpreted in this way. The important thing is that people's equal interests are given equal consideration when the utilitarian calculation is done. The potential for a successful outcome, however, clearly cannot be an irrelevant consideration within a utilitarian framework.

Our consideration of utility points to two main factors insufficiently catered for: we cannot ignore the need for some criterion of distribution; and we cannot ignore the moral urgency of people's suffering. A just society is not one that abandons people to their fate.

The second point suggests that what is needed is a broader concept of benefit, or medical success. Thus Doyal says: "When [patients'] situations are acute, their right of access to health care is strengthened because of their need. It should be, however, to a different type of care, one which recognises the futility of continuing clinical management which pretends to be curative when it cannot be."[14] This comment, while not saying so explicitly, points us to the fact that there may be different kinds of benefit. A poor prognosis does not entail that little or no benefit is possible.

Conclusions

None of the above conceptions of justice gives us an adequate theory of priority setting on its own. Daniels is right to say that more work needs to be done at the theoretical level to resolve the problems outlined above.

As far as the desert model is concerned, it is acceptable to encourage individual responsibility for health, but not to use it as a criterion for denying resources. A just society will surely give people what they need, but in the light of the priorities problem this has to be tempered by some consideration of the possibilities of medical success. Medical success alone, however, potentially ignores distribution problems and the suffering of the disease state. What would be desirable would be a bridge between these two, so that need provides a criterion of distribution to utility, and utility provides success to need. This bridge might seem to be encapsulated in the attempt to define need as capacity to benefit, but this is not sufficient. To define need in terms of capacity to benefit is a different thing from using utility as a criterion for prioritising between needs previously identified. If we cannot meet everyone's needs, we should face up to this. It is unacceptable to try to define away people's problems. Nord has shown the importance of not ignoring a person's actual state before treatment, and Doyal is right to point out that people for whom the prognosis is very poor are still in need: someone may still be in need although intervention may not seem likely to offer much utility under QALY interpretation. So at the very least, in attempting to build a bridge between the need and utility conceptions of justice as applied to health care, concepts of need and of benefit which take these points into account will be required.

1 Kant I. *Critique of pure reason.* London: Macmillan, 1970: A807, B835. (First published 1787; trans. Norman Kemp Smith.)
2 Rawls J. *A theory of justice.* Boston: Harvard University Press, 1971: 62.
3 Daniels N. Rationing fairly: programmatic considerations. *Bioethics* 1993; 7: 224–33.
4 Gallie WB. Essentially contested concepts. *Proceedings of the Aristotelian Society* 1955–6; 56: 167–98.
5 Hunt RW, Callahan D. Debate: a critique of using age to ration health care. *J Med Ethics* 1993; 19: 19–27.
6 Campbell T. *Justice.* Basingstoke: Macmillan, 1988: 151–2; 155–6.
7 *Choices in health care: a report by the government committee on choices in health care.* Rijswijk,

Netherlands: Ministry of Health, Welfare, and Cultural Affairs, 1992. (AJ Dunning, chairman.)

8 Williams B. The idea of equality. In: *Problems of the self*. Cambridge: Cambridge University Press, 1973: 240.

9 Miller D. *Social justice*. Oxford: Clarendon Press, 1976: 149.

10 Raphael DD. *Moral philosophy*. Oxford: Oxford University Press, 1981: 71.

11 Baker J. *Arguing for equality* London: Verso, 1987: 61–4.

12 Williams MH, Frankel SJ. The myth of infinite demand. *Critical Public Health*. 1993: 4: 13–8.

13 Hadorn DC. The Oregon priority-setting exercise: quality of life and public policy. *Hastings Center Report*. 1991: 21: (suppl): 11–6.

14 Doyal L. The role of the public in health care rationing. *Critical Public Health*. 1993: 4: 49–54.

15 Veatch RM. Should basic care get priority? Doubts about rationing the Oregon way. *Kennedy Institute of Ethics Journal* 1993: 1: 187–206.

16 Hunter DJ. Rationing and health gain. *Critical Public Health* 1993: 4: 27–33.

17 Hare RM. What is wrong with slavery? *Philosophy and Public Affairs* 1979: 8: 103–21.

18 Kappel K, Sandøe P. QALYs, age and fairness. *Bioethics* 1992: 6: 297–316.

19 Harris J. QALYfying the value of life. *J Med Ethics* 1987: 13: 117–23.

20 Nord E. An alternative to QALYs: the saved young life equivalent (SAVE). *BMJ* 1992: 305: 875–7.

21 Nord E. The relevance of health state after treatment in prioritising different patients. *J Med Ethics* 1993: 19: 37–42.

9 Dimensions of rationing: who should do what?

RUDOLF KLEIN

My starting point is the all pervasive nature of priority setting in all health care systems. Decisions about how to allocate resources— what we call, if we want to raise the emotional level of the debate, rationing—take place at all levels of the organisational hierarchy and the delivery system. Everyone in any health care system is (to exaggerate only a little) taking decisions about how best to prior- itise resources all the time. The process starts from the moment I enter my doctor's surgery. The receptionist takes a decision, when I ask for an appointment, about how urgent my case is: what Roy Parker called, in a seminal article published 25 years ago, rationing by deterrence or delay.[1] When I eventually get to see my doctor, he or she will decide whether to give me five minutes or ten. Next will come a decision about whether or not to refer me to hospital (unless I short circuit the whole process by having a heart attack). Then I may or may not be put on a waiting list, and eventually—if I survive rationing by delay and depending on my priority rating— I may get to be treated in hospital. While I am there, doctors will take decisions about just what resources to throw at me—rationing by dilution, in Parker's terminology—and just how many tests and investigations to order. Finally, there will be decisions about how long to keep me in hospital: rationing by termination of treatment.

Two things need to be noted about this process. Firstly, all the micro decisions about priority setting are constrained by macro decisions about resource allocation taken at superior levels in the organisational hierarchy: decisions in the Cabinet about how much to allocate to the NHS, decisions by the Department of Health

96

about what priority targets to set to health authorities, and finally decisions by purchasers about what services to buy. Secondly, all the micro decisions are taken in terms of "need" as interpreted by the professional providers, notably the medical profession—that is, the perceived level of severity and urgency. Need, we have to recognise, is both an imprecise and an elastic concept, variously interpreted by different practitioners:[2] hence, of course, the frequently observed and much commented on variations in referral and operating rates.[3]

Multiple decisions for allocating resources

So when we talk about priority setting we are really discussing the complex interaction of multiple decisions, taken at various levels in the organisation, about allocating resources. The secretary of state for health, Mrs Bottomley, could doubtless make the task of priority setting for doctors somewhat easier if she winkled out more funds for the NHS, though it is dangerous to assume that there would be no need for rationing if only Britain spent a higher proportion of the national income on health care. The case of the Netherlands provides a warning on this point: the Netherlands spent 8% of its gross domestic product on health care in 1990, in comparison to the United Kingdom's 6.2%[4], yet it is currently debating what should and should not be included in the services provided—witness the publication of the Dunning report.[5] Conversely, the medical profession could make Mrs Bottomley's life much more pleasant by putting fewer people on the waiting lists (not a self evidently absurd proposition, given that there are no nationally agreed criteria for treatment and considerable evidence of variations in thresholds used by different consultants). To exaggerate only a little, demand for health care is what the medical profession chooses to make it: the pace at which it introduces new technologies, the rate at which is adopts new procedures, and so on.

Moreover, we are talking about decisions constrained by history: the inherited pattern of distribution between different sectors of the NHS and between different specialties. Priority setting is, inescapably, an incremental process. It involves decisions about how to spend the annual budgetary increment or how to react to budget cuts. In theory it may possible to reallocate existing resources—to start from a clean slate and adopt a strategy of zero based budgeting—but in practice institutional resistance makes it difficult to do so on a large scale or in the short term. The constituency for the status quo tends to be powerful in health care, as in other services. Those who benefit from the existing pattern of service provision, whether as providers or consumers, tend to be concentrated and organised advocates for maintaining it, while those who stand to gain from the reallocation of funds are, by definition, a diffuse and difficult to identify group. The point is well illustrated by an analysis of the 1992-3 purchasing plans carried out at Bath,[6] as part of a larger study of resource allocation policies in the NHS funded by the Nuffield Provincial Hospitals Trust. This showed a general reluctance to choose between competing claims on resources, with little evidence of explicit rationing (in the sense of limiting the menu of services offered by the NHS) or of any willingness to make dramatic changes. To the extent that the purchasers were prepared to modify the existing distribution of resources, it was very much at the margins. They tended to pursue a policy of "spreading the money around"—that is, of keeping as many people as possibly happy by giving them some funds—even if this meant giving them only token amounts.

There is nothing surprising about such findings. They are very much in line with what would be expected on the basis both of theory and of the NHS's practice over the past 40 years. But it may be possible to draw out some less obvious implications. My starting point in doing this is the contention that there is no self evident set of ethical principles or of analytic tools which allows us to determine what sort of decisions we should take at different levels in the organisation. Consider, first, the question of what priority the government should give to health care when considering competing claims on resources. No one has yet come up with a convincing method for determining how much should be spent on the NHS. Much has been made of the famous 2% formula, the contention that the NHS needs an annual increment of 2% in its budget to cope with demographic and technological change. But this is based on extrapolating past trends and does not tell us anything about the adequacy or otherwise of the baseline from which the calculations start. Nor do comparisons with other countries help much. If another country spends a higher proportion of the national income on health care it may be because it is providing more health care or because each unit of service produced is more expensive or, come to that, because it is spending too

A machine for grinding out priorities is absurd

much on ineffective procedures. And some nations—notably Denmark and Japan—spend much the same proportion as Britain without seemingly perceiving their health care systems to be under funded and suffering from the kind of periodic crises that have afflicted the NHS since its birth.

Distributing the budget

Moving, next, to decisions about how to distribute the total budget among services, there is once again no obvious or easy way of resolving the clash of claims on resources.[7] Quality adjusted life years (QALYs), as even the advocates of this decision making tool concede, are at best aids to decision making, providing an input of information. They are beset by methodological problems about the valuation of different states of health, by lack of data about outcomes, and by the problem of patient heterogeneity (the fact that the benefits of any given procedure may vary greatly among patients). Public opinion surveys are extraordinarily sensitive to the way in which questions are put and raise worrying issues about what weight should be put to answers given without any contextual information. Moreover, "the public" is a complex notion. As consumers of health care we may well have different priorities from those we have as citizens, just as there may be well be differences between the consumers and the providers.[8] We could say, of course, that priority should always be given to procedures that are demonstrably effective over those that are not. It is difficult to disagree with this proposition, but I am not sure how far this gets us given the extent of our ignorance about effectiveness. Similarly, we could say that priority should follow need. But, again, how far does this get us, given the ambiguity of the concept? Moreover, if it is difficult to devise acceptable principles for prioritising medical interventions (the curing or repair function of the NHS), the problem is compounded when we address questions about allocating resources to the caring function of any health care system and the management of chronic conditions.

Making priority setting more "rational"

All this may suggest that the argument is moving towards the despairing conclusion that there is no "rational" way of determining priorities: that, like it or not, we are still left with priorities emerging from pluralistic bargaining between different lobbies, modified by shifting political judgments made in the light of changing pressures. To an extent, indeed, that is my conclusion. But I would like to argue, firstly, that such a conclusion is not as negative as so often assumed and, secondly, that there is scope for making the process of priority setting more "rational."

My first contention is that, given the plurality of often conflicting values that can be brought to any discussion of priorities in health care, it is positively undesirable (as well as foolish) to search for some set of principles or techniques that will make our decisions for us: the idea of a machine for grinding out priorities is absurd. What is so often wrong about pluralistic bargaining is that it is not pluralistic enough: that discussion is dominated by some voices (notably those of the medical profession). Similarly, pluralistic bargaining often tends to confuse arguments based on interests with those based on values (although most of us have a highly developed capacity for translating our self interest into the high flown language of values).

From this follows my second point, which is that if we are concerned to make priority setting somehow more "rational" (a

> ## Dimensions of rationing
> - Priority setting is a complex interaction of multiple decisions at various levels in the organisation and constrained by history
> - There is no self evident set of ethical principles or analytical tools to determine what decisions we should take at various levels
> - There is no obvious or easy way to resolve the clash of claims on resources
> - To make priority setting more "rational" we should concentrate on the processes and structure of decision making, and the relation of macro and micro decisions
> - The debate should promote reasoned, informed, and open argument, draw on a variety of perspectives, and involve a plurality of interests
> - Our aim must be to build up, over time, our capacity to engage in continuous, collective argument

dangerous word, anyway), we should concentrate on the processes of decision making. Rationality, from this perspective, lies in creating a situation in which there is open dialogue, in which opportunities for taking part in debate are widely distributed, in which arguments can be tested against evidence and the conflicts between different values or preferences can be explored. It is a concept of rationality which goes back to Aristotle[9] and which puts the emphasis on finding "good reasons" to justify decisions. And it is an approach which, I would argue, leads us out of the dead end of searching for some over arching formula for determining priorities by directing our attention to the *structure* of decision making.

The structure of decision making

Taking this approach, the question then becomes: how far does the present structure of decision making allow rational argument (in the sense of reasoned and open discussion) about priorities? So we might start at the top of the decision making hierarchy and ask how the secretary of state and her department reach—and can justify—their priorities. We might further ask what criteria and evidence are used to come to such decisions about the allocation of resources: the balance between political expediency, cost-benefit considerations, and other factors. Next we might probe the extent

101

to which other actors—such as the House of Commons health committee—can challenge and test the way in which the department formulates its policies. Are there enough opportunities for putting the department on the rack of cross examination and exploring alternative options?

Moving down one step in the organisational hierarchy, we might ask much the same sort of questions about purchasers. What assumptions, evidence, and criteria shape the policies about priorities? Which interests are represented in the decision making arena and, equally important, who is excluded? If public opinion surveys do not necessarily make much of a contribution to reasoned argument, although they may contribute some raw material, are there other ways in which purchasers test out their own plans and offer an opportunity to others to challenge their arguments and presumptions? Is the process of priority setting transparent enough?

Similarly, moving to the micro level of decision making, we can ask about the processes by which clinicians prioritise between the competing claims on resources and on their time. What criteria do they use in determining entry to, and progress up, waiting lists? What are their definitions of "need," and what weight do they give to different considerations—such as the age of the patient, the costs and effectiveness of different types of treatment, or the social implications of delay? And, again, we might ask to what extent such decisions are open to challenge: whether, for example, medical audit is an adequate instrument for testing different clinical policies and priorities. Should clinicians have to justify their judgments about priorities—about whom to treat, at what level of intensity—to a wider audience?

Finally, we should be concerned about the relationship between macro and micro decisions: in particular the feedback between the different levels in the organisational hierarchy. It is not self evident that at present there is adequate information about how broad macro decisions about priorities, taken at the top of the hierarchy, translate into clinical decisions at the bottom about who should be treated and how. Again, waiting lists provide a classic example: lacking any evidence about the criteria used for giving priority to different patients, we simply do not know whether lengthening queues mean that the threshold of admission has been lowered or whether they imply that access is being delayed or denied to patients who previously would have been treated. Yet, in the absence of such information, how can there be rational argument about the government's priorities?

The structure of the debate

My argument then, to sum up, is that there is no technological fix, scientific method, or method of philosophic inquiry for determining priorities. Of course, the three E's—economists, ethicists, and epidemiologists—all have valuable insights to contribute to the debate about resource allocation and rationing, though none of them can resolve our dilemmas for us. But what really matters is how that debate is structured: how far it promotes reasoned, informed, and open argument, drawing on a variety of perspectives and involving a plurality of interests. The debate about priorities will never be finally resolved. Nor should we expect any final resolution. As medical technology, the economic and demographic environment, and social attitudes change, so almost certainly will our priorities. And we have to recognise that much of medicine is about the management of uncertainty, where research may roll back the frontiers of ignorance but is never likely to eliminate totally the need for clinical discretion and the use of judgment in interpreting the evidence about efficacy and outcomes.

Our aim must therefore be to build up, over time, our capacity to engage in continuous, collective argument. This means, in turn, devising institutions that encourage, rather than discourage, challenge, allow the implications of pursuing different priorities to be tested out, and provide the information required for reasoned debate. In short, we should be at least as much concerned with the structure of our institutions, and the way in which they work, as with the development of techniques. The politics of priority setting (in the widest sense) matter as much as the methodologies used.

This is very much a recipe for the long haul, but it is one that acknowledges the multidimensional complexity of priority setting. It is precisely this complexity which does not allow any easy or quick solutions and which forces us to accept (however reluctantly) that this is a voyage of discovery where we will never reach a final destination. To put it another way, this is an argument that will never be finally settled, but in which we can try at least to ensure that it is conducted with due concern about openness, the appropriate use of evidence, and attention to what counts as good currency in the debate.

This paper draws on research on priority setting in the NHS funded by the Nuffield Provincial Hospitals Trust.

1 Parker R. Social administration and scarcity. Reprinted in: Butterworth E, Holman R. eds. *Social welfare in modern britain*. London: Fontana, 1975, 204–12.
2. Cooper MH. *Rationing health care*. London: Croom Helm, 1975.
3. Ham C. ed. *Health care variations*. London: King's Fund Institute, 1988.
4. Organisation for Economic Cooperation and Development. *The reform of health care*. Paris: OECD, 1992.
5. *Report of the government committee on choices in health care*. Rijswijk: Ministry of Welfare, Health and Cultural Affairs, 1992. (AJ Dunning, chairman)
6. Klein R, Redmayne S. *Patterns of priorities*. Birmingham: National Association of Health Authorities and Trusts, 1992.
7. Hunter D. *Rationing dilemmas in health care*. Birmingham: National Association of Health Authorities and Trusts, 1993.
8. Groves T. Public disagrees with professionals over NHS rationing. *BMJ* 1993; **306**: 673.
9. Beiner R. *Political judgment*. Chicago: University of Chicago Press, 1983.

PART IV: THE PLAYERS

10 Surely you aren't going to ration *me*!

KATHARINE WHITEHORN

A patient is in somewhat the same situation as the man who said that he knew all men were mortal, but that he'd always understood an exception would be made in his case. If a woman's husband is terribly ill, she's not going to say that it's hardly worth his having a £50 000 transplant (if she does, you've got some other questions to ask); a couple whose baby is poorly inevitably says, "Doctor, do anything—*anything*—to save our baby." But that doesn't mean it's the right thing to do, even from the baby's point of view; just as, if you are falling off a cliff, you naturally grab any branch that's offered, though there's actually no guarantee that you are better off hanging in mid-air for hours before you finally give up and crash onto the rocks below. No one can take anything but an individual and panic-stricken view of an immediate crisis; but that is not priority setting.

So what can patients be persuaded to accept? If the illness simply has no cure, they can ultimately accept it, just as the old islander who was asked what on earth they did before the helicopter service: what happened when they were dangerously ill? "We mostly died," he said calmly. My father has had a heart attack; the baby is born dead; the cancer is inoperable: that is as acceptable as death has ever been. And the situation is not that different when a cure is one a patient would not normally expect. Thirty years ago a transplant wasn't an option; a hundred years ago tuberculosis was something to which you had to become resigned; even nowadays we in Britain don't expect to give renal dialysis to a 90 year old—though they do in the United States, simply because someone

107

demonstrated a dialysis machine on the floor of Congress and the representatives all rose up and said every last one of their constituents must have it.

But when what has to be said is, in effect, "We could cure you but we won't because we can't afford it," that's a very different matter. Patients need to believe that their doctors are doing all they humanly can; it is a very rare—and enlightened—patient who can ever say, "I'd rather die straightforwardly than go for a one in a hundred chance with tubes up my nose and my hair falling out." And here you have a difficulty: the quasireligious aura that surrounds doctors may make it easier for them to say "There is nothing we can do" and have it accepted; but no such aura surrounds administrators or the Department of Health. At the slightest suspicion of being left to die—or left in pain, sleepless, aching, rocking on your bedsores—because the bureaucrats can't get their sums right, any patient's condition is immediately worsened by a blind rage. No wonder one hospital sent out a directive to say that patients were not to be "bothered by politics," by which it meant that if an operation was postponed the patients weren't to be told that it was because the health authority had run out of money. "You can't be cured because we haven't got the money" is not, after all, all that far away from "You can't be cured because *you* haven't got the money"—which, every time we look across the Atlantic, we find outrageous.

Self help

If the panicky patient at the moment of misery can't sensibly determine what is and isn't worth doing, who can? Their self help groups would say that they could; and certainly they know what their groups of sufferers feel: they know a great deal, the single disease groups, about what treatments work, what help other than treatment (home adaptations for the handicapped, alternative medicines, respite help for exhausted carers, and so on) their people need. They may inadvertently help the cash strapped health service by pointing out that something fashionable and expensive isn't any good, but they are not actually much good at rationing. (Why not call it what it is? Rationing in wartime is introduced so that the way food is doled out shall be fair. Not such a bad idea.) They are partial and blinkered, in exactly the same way as the desperate individual; they think, inevitably, that their illness is the one that really matters most. As do, of course, the specialist consultants: the heart man who wants every schoolchild trained in resuscitation, and ambulances quartering the countryside at all hours; the neurologist who needs ever more sensitive machines—their claims are just, but they aren't the people to balance them against all the other claims.

That goes, too, for all the various charities concerned with the aged. Maybe elderly people do get a raw deal, though I'm inclined to think it is worse to be kept alive too long than to go too soon. I am horrified to hear the beginning of a groundswell of protest against "agism" in medicine. That the old shouldn't be written off, or their ailments put down to "just age" and ignored, I would of course agree; but that we should struggle to keep really old people alive in the same way and with the same vigour as those in the prime of life seems to me senseless—and I think I have a right to say this, since I'm old enough to put not just MA and LLD after my name but DNR. And of course it's the same at the other end of life, struggling to keep ever tinier babies going, whatever their prospects. No society can save every last fetus, or keep every citizen going to the age of 120.

Public preferences

So if it isn't the patients or their special interest groups who should decide on priorities, who is it? General organisations that serve patients' interests *generally* should have a part in the argument—community health councils, general groups like the Patients Association; perhaps local groups like friends of the hospital (though beware of their favouring the speciality for which their hospital happens to have a reputation); specially convened meetings and seminars are useful, perhaps. The snag about widely trawled public expressions of preference is that people can only choose between options they've actually heard of—and they've what heard about tends to be what they've read in the newspapers. Hence there is an inevitable bias towards the dramatic: hole in the heart baby, mercy dash, life saving drug—they have been bombarded with all that, not with the debilitating degenerative diseases, or the miseries of being deaf as opposed to blind, or the grey mudflats of depressive illness.

As a member of the press I naturally try to look on its bright side, but I realise only too well that the press has a built-in bias towards the spectacular, the interesting. But there it is; you wouldn't read headlines like "Many thousands use chiropody services" or "Lower back pain relief at risk." One sentence that for me stood out like a banner in the sky was Rudolf Klein's doubt about "the weight to be attached to opinions not based on information." It does cast rather a doubt on democracy, but that's another matter.

Consider the patient

I was very glad to hear scepticism about limiting treatment for those whose sickness was deemed to be their own fault, for I really loathe the idea of the Deserving Patient. For one thing, fashions in this sort of their change: we may be reasonably certain now that tobacco is bad for you, but what about the shifting tides of opinion on cholesterol? Suppose you had been withholding treatment from people who'd been incontinently eating butter? But the even more important point is that you may be able to tell that someone has an unhealthy lifestyle, but not how good their chances were of ever avoiding it—not unless you, too, have been a single parent cooped up with three children and an inadequate boyfriend, say, or coping alone with a malicious old parent. It was Herman Melville who said: "Of all the preposterous assumptions of humanity over humanity, nothing exceeds most of the criticisms made on the habits of the poor by the well-housed, well-warmed and well-fed." Please don't let us drag that into medicine.

Perhaps the final thing that needs saying is to emphasise, yet again, the gulf that has to be bridged between the patient and the point of view of everyone concerned with rationing of health care. You are concerned, informed, active, with careers to make in the health service, aware that tough decisions have to be made, but not at the receiving end of them. The patient is upset, powerless, possibly frightened, and not feeling at all well. "The toad beneath the harrow knows/Where each spoke of that harrow goes./The butterfly upon the road/Preaches contentment to the Toad." I leave you to decide who, in this scenario, are the butterflies.

11 You are all my patients

BRIAN GOSS

We will never know the true motivation behind *Working for Patients*, but even the most committed Thatcherite has never claimed that it was devised as a mechanism for pouring vast sums of money into the NHS, and it is certainly possible to view the reforms as a cynical ploy to gain even better control over the health care budget and exert "downward pressure" on funding while ensuring that the blame for the results is able to be distanced from government—and preferably landed at the door of the general practitioner.

Can general practitioners generally, and fundholders in particular, operate rationing and let everyone else (but especially politicians) off the hook? This is the question that I, as a representative of ordinary working general practitioners, will address.

There are two jobs to be done in health care rationing. Prioritisation is the first task, but the second may be more important; it consists of advocacy for the individual, and for the healthcare budget itself. I accept that almost no amount of expenditure on health would be considered adequate by some, but I do not accept that the proportion of Britain's gross domestic product now devoted to health has been handed down on tablets of stone. This proportion is among the lowest in the developed world (fig 1), and 20 years' personal experience of the operation of the NHS does not convince me that this level of expenditure is adequate to provide a basic and decent level of health care, even with every efficiency saving possible.

When I think of rationing, then, I ask myself two questions—

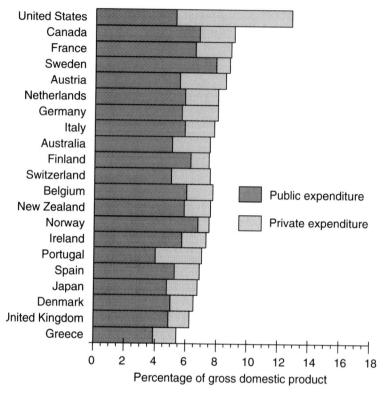

FIG 1—Expenditure on health as percentage of gross domestic product

how can we order priorities to the best effect with today's resources, and how can we use information from the current system
to obtain more real resources for tomorrow. Of these two, the
second is by far the more important, and my support for the NHS
reforms and the internal market is entirely founded in the belief
that, by being a system based on explicit rather than implicit
rationing, it renders government more politically vulnerable and
better NHS funding more likely

General practitioners have an important role in advocacy and an
essential role in advising on strategic priorities. But they are not
likely to be as good as a few of them may be thinking at individual
rationing in times of scarcity.

First of all, much of the point of rationing is to provoke the
public into "choosing" to dig deeper into its private pocket for that

112

which the NHS does not provide. This is emotionally unacceptable to most general practitioners, who have repeatedly passed resolutions at annual representative meetings proclaiming commitment to a comprehensive NHS free at the point of delivery, and any reversal of this policy would go to the heart of the deep seated commitment which evoked Tudor-Hart's observation on his retirement: "The NHS has allowed me to treat my patients during an entire working lifetime, without ever having to collect a fee."

In pointing out the probable historical uniqueness of that experience, Tudor-Hart identifies a feature of an entire medical workforce which, for all the cynical jokes, has a genuine and deep seated commitment to the system which protects it from the ugly fact that nearly all other doctors in history have had to face— namely, that physicians have to make their living by adding a bill to the misfortune, anxiety, and suffering of other human beings. We should think carefully before reversing that attitude, which owes as much to the moral rectitude of British doctors as it does to 40 years' experience of the NHS.

GPs rationing their own work

Let us look at general practitioners in rationing their own work before examining them as "gatekeepers." General practitioners are certainly aware that they cannot forever sustain from their own energies those rising expectations which are legitimised under the current regulatory definition of general practice, which says (with apologies to John Wayne) "a GP's gotta do what GPs do."

At some stage, surely, people must be prepared to bring private expenditure into the health service to pay for certain non-lifesaving services? Last year's *Building your own Future* survey by the General Medical Services Committee, however, showed that the vast majority of general practitioners did not support any form of charging patients, even for such services as non-emergency out of hours care, which they found most irksome to deliver.[2] The time may not be far off, though, when the rising clamour of public expectation, combined with a reluctance to fund the service out of taxation, forces a change in general practitioners' attitude to patient charges.

Explicit rationing of general practice itself would be difficult and unacceptable to general practitioners today, but by no means impossible. One approach may be to use an Oregon-style system

113

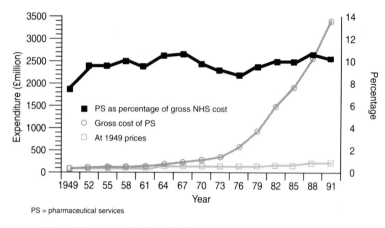

FIG 2—Cost of pharmaceutical services in the United Kingdom

based on diagnosis related groups and to allow reimbursement of consultation fees only for defined conditions. Such a system not only reflects more accurately than simple capitation the workload generated by individual patients, but it sits well with organised care based on clinical guidelines. Perhaps surprisingly, American experience has tended not to confirm early expectations that doctors would "play the system" by coding more remunerative diagnoses.

GPs as rationers

Prescribing costs are rising at a rate that terrifies the government but is not surprising to practitioners faced with ingredient cost inflation, demographic change, and dumping of hospital prescribing. In addition, rational scientific prescribing increasingly requires good doctors to prescribe more expensive drugs such as angiotensin converting enzyme inhibitors, inhaled steroids, and anticancer agents. Against that background it is the flatness of the lines showing measures of "real" cost that is surprising, not the gradient of the one showing cash values, which tells us more about inflation than prescribing (fig 2).

In the face of the unequivocal regulatory requirement that a doctor shall order all necessary treatment, downward pressure on

114

prescribing costs can be delivered only if those doctors who already prescribe rationally have the legal cover to say no. Enter the limited list.

Despite initial opposition from both the profession and the pharmaceutical industry, the introduction of the limited list scheme in 1985 left no bodies in the streets, and it proved to be an area of explicit rationing which general practitioners can readily if unenthusiastically administer, since they can distance themselves from the decision and displace blame to government, where it belongs.

If general practitioners are able to administer only the most explicit forms of rationing in prescribing, how do they fare as rationers of hospital and other secondary services?

Referral—commissioning secondary care

General practitioner fundholding is seen by some as the answer to resourcing problems. Closer analysis reveals, however, that the greatest successes of fundholding have been in the fields of negotiating adequate funding, and then bludgeoning hospitals into operating on the patients who general practitioners consider deserving.

Such economies in secondary care as fundholders have been able to make have largely been in releasing patients from unnecessary hospital follow up. Otherwise they have not yet had to ration hospital services on any scale. This is largely because, in general, providers have lacked either the capacity or the will to absorb such funds as the fundholders are offering. But the signs are already there that the situation is changing.

The 1993–4 budget offers were generally lower in real terms than in previous years. It will be interesting to see whether the doctors respond as bankrupt district health authorities have, by rationing, or by overspending. My prediction is that most will overspend rather than confront individual patients with the fact that the budgetary allocation has run out. This is surely the appropriate course for a group of doctors proud of their advocacy on behalf of patients, and it is all the more predictable because doctors have to face individual patients and are subject to obligations that do not apply to district health authorities.

Patient participation

In my fundholding practice we have had the very considerable benefit of advice on priorities and purchasing from a patient participation group formed specifically for managing the fund. Patient participation groups cannot, of course, ethically become involved in discussions about individual patients, but we have engaged the group in discussions about the relative priorities to be given to different procedures and treatments—a sort of Oregon experiment scaled down to the size of a small Suffolk market town.

As resources become more constrained such discussions may well lead our patient group to encourage doctors to be more frugal in their referral behaviour. In practice I suspect that the reverse may be the case, and the current terms of service of general practitioners certainly do not facilitate rationing. Instead general practitioners are required to refer when necessary and with no reference to the availability of resources.

Complaints by patients against general practitioners frequently involve alleged failure to refer or treat under this unequivocal regulation, but I have yet to come across one where a patient alleges that the doctor has been profligate in the use of NHS resources. Indeed, in my area not only has the number of complaints increased substantially in the past two years but over the past five the traditional "failure to visit" has diminished and been replaced by "failure to refer." Had every doctor in the land adopted the referral policy implicitly required by the complainant, the hospital services would have ground to a halt long ago.

Therefore I cannot see general practitioners helping to avoid explicit rationing in referral any more than in prescribing. But, on the same basis, a limited list of procedures ordained by regulations which, like the limited list rule, protects general practitioners who follow them is feasible.

A role for GPs in rationing

So what is the role, if any, for general practitioners? Whether fundholders or not, they can offer, and increasingly are offering, valuable and practical advice to health authorities on strategic aspects of purchasing. They can advise on the ordering of priorities and the criteria for explicit rationing when it is necessary. But both the purchasing authorities and the funding authorities for fundholders need to recognise the parallel advocacy role which general practitioners must fulfil, both for individuals and the community at large, as being part of their integrity and not duplicity.

The average general practitioner, remember, gets through a quarter of a million consultations, a thousand births and deaths, and fifteen secretaries of state for health in a professional lifetime. So general practitioners' feet are on the ground, and their loyalty is to the patient.

General practitioners, both as fundholders and as non-fund-holders advising purchasing authorities, have the potential to become a potent political force in securing the allocation of proper levels of resource to the NHS from all shades of future government. Doctors who are hospital employees are under increasing contractual restraints regarding their freedom to enter public debate. As independent contractors who are proud of their traditional role of patient advocacy, general practitioners are well placed to form partnerships with patients that can assess need, order priorities, and command public attention if resourcing levels fall short of what is required to provide a comprehensive NHS free at the point of delivery. Those partnerships will, of course, deliver only if the public is truly minded to support the NHS financially as well as morally.

Explicit rationing combined with the realisation that the share of gross domestic product allocated to health care is not a divinely determined figure could put the resource allocation cudgel into the hands of a patient-professional partnership rather than the hands of politicians. It is up to the public, through government, to decide on the sort of health service it wishes to afford to deserve.

1 Tudor-Hart J. *A new kind of doctor*. London: Merlin Press, 1988.
2 General Medical Services Committee. *Building your own future*. London: GMSC, 1992.

12 This patient or that patient?

JOHN GRIMLEY EVANS

"Priority setting" is Newspeak for "rationing." There are three levels of health care rationing in the public sector: the first lies in setting the proportion of national income to be dedicated to health care; the second is concerned with the types of health care to be bought with that money; the third lies with deciding who is to receive what is available. Although rationing has the inevitable implication of deprivation, it acquired during the second world war the implication of equity, and it is this aspect of rationing, the essence of the Shavian doctor's dilemma, that concerns clinicians most closely.

An important element in the difficulties of rationing is the temptation to treat individuals merely as members of arbitrarily defined groups. It is a paradox in our culture that, although we regard ourselves as individualist, appreciate eccentricity, and believe our social structures to be aimed at fostering individualism, we are all too ready to classify people into groups and treat them as though they were homogeneous. The drive to categorisation of people may be intensified in Britain by the residual memory of a class system, but categorisation itself is a long established tradition of Western thought.

A question of age?

Age is a useful probe for identifying the kinds of illogicality and injustice that can arise from categorisation. There is abundant

118

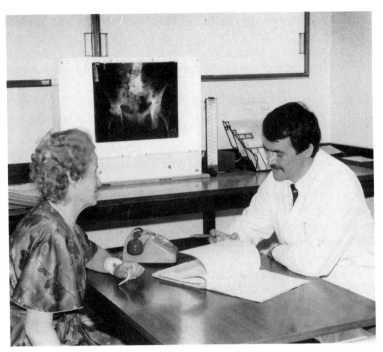

FIG 1—Older people who are taught defensive health behaviour are advised to treat their doctor as a learned moron who will be able to help them only if they put their complaints into words that he can understand

evidence of agism in the health services in that older people get offered worse care than do younger adults. In the United States, for example, it has been documented that doctors spend less time with older patients even though, on average, the health problems of older people are more complex.[1] Indeed, there has developed a proposal in the United States for defensive health behaviour, in which old people are to be taught how to get good health care in spite of a delivery system that is weighted against them.[2] In defensive health behaviour older people are advised, for example, to treat their doctor as a learned moron who will be able to help them only if they put their complaints into words that he or she can understand.

The quality of care offered to cancer patients varies with age, with older people on average being offered worse and less effective treatment.[3] In Britain it has been well known that the treatment of

119

renal failure is agist in its distribution compared with most European countries. In the mid-1980s only 8% of patients receiving dialysis in Britain were aged over 65, compared with around 25% in Germany, France, and Italy.[4] This is despite a five year survival rate of 62% in the older people compared with 44% in patients aged 55 to 64. Moreover, as colleagues in Oxford have shown, in terms of quality of life the results of dialysis for patients aged over 60 may actually be better than for younger patients.[5]

Agist discrimination has also been documented in Britain with regard to investigation and treatment of heart disease. In one study it was shown that older people coming to coronary angiography were on average more ill than the younger patients undergoing similar investigation.[6] This compounds any association of age with outcome since the more severe the patient's illness, the poorer his or her prospects, and if patients are left to deteriorate they may have to undergo emergency procedures, which carry additional excess fatality.

In a much quoted study Dudley and Burns showed that 19% of coronary care units in Britain have an upper age limit varying upwards from 65 for admission.[7] There is no evidence that older people with acute heart attacks benefit less than younger people from specialist cardiological care, but in many health districts in Britain patients over an arbitrary age with heart attacks are sent to geriatric departments rather than medical or cardiological units. Even worse, the Dudley and Burns study found that 40% of districts have an upper age limit for thrombolytic treatment. This is worse than unjust, it is illogical, since data from the large international study of infarct survival (ISIS) trial showed that in terms of lives saved per 1000 patients treated, thrombolytic treatment is more than twice as effective if given to patients aged over 70 than to patients under 55.[8]

All these are examples of what has been called "aggravated aging."[9] Because you expect old people to do badly you do not notice that they are doing worse than they need because you are treating them badly.

Poor science and woolly ethics

This situation been allowed to come about because of poor science and woolly ethics. Doctors may claim justification for

120

excluding older patients from treatments on the grounds that older patients do not benefit, but this is known not to be the case for some common disorders. For others we do not know whether it is the case or not because older people are all too often excluded from the trials of new treatments. The only reason we know that thrombolytic treatment is more effective in old people is because one of the Oxford investigators insisted on people over 70 being included in the ISIS-2 trial even though several previous studies had excluded them. Treatment trials are still being funded for diseases that affect older people but from which older people are excluded.

A second excuse for withholding treatment from older people is an alleged high risk of side effects. Again, this has often not been tested, and as we have seen for peritoneal dialysis the impact of side effects on quality of life may actually be lower for older patients. For some other treatments, such as anticoagulant therapy, any tendency towards a higher risk of side effects for older people and some other groups of patients can be easily offset by more assiduous care and supervision of dosage.

There is also muddled scientific thought about age as a causative variable. Age is an abstract number; in itself it cannot actually cause anything, although it is a familiar category error to speak and think as if it could. The reason that age may be associated, on average, with differences in outcome from treatment is because of the prevalence of physiological impairments, which increases with age. We do not all accumulate physiological impairments, and for most variables there is an appreciable percentage of people aged 80 still functioning with the normal range for people aged 30. Scientific logic requires that we should not regard older people merely as members of the group of "the elderly" or as "geriatrics" but rather think about their health problems as individuals. We would not countenance exclusion from optimal treatment of the lower social classes or blacks, though in these groups, as in older people, there is on average poorer outcome from health interventions than in upper class whites. We should aim to acquire enough information to be able to work out for each person, regardless of age, what the cost-benefit ratio of a contemplated intervention would be. If we pursue this aim we may expect that more older people in Britain will receive beneficial care that is at present being withheld from them. Conversely, we may expect that some younger people might be spared futile but expensive and unpleasant treatment (for malignant disease, for example) that is at present unthinkingly imposed on them simply because they are young.

Ethics and ideology

In discussing these matters we are in the borderlands between science and ethics, and as regards health care we are at present in something of a muddle about ethics. There cannot be an ethics without a system of ideological values from which ethical principles of behaviour are logical deductions. Those who offer opinions on ethics without declaring the ideology from which they are working are usually trying to sell something. Is there an ideology in British society that transcends the two and seventy jarring sects of a multicultural nation? We do not have a consititution, we do not have a bill of rights, but most indigenous Britons assume that there is an ideology that characterises British society. It has to do with vague ideas such as the sanctity, equality, and autonomy of the individual. We cannot deduce a national ideology from the law, which is merely the product of the fears of politicians and the greed of lawyers, and nor can we expect to deduce it by asking the "man in the street." In a recent study respondents in Cardiff were presented with a series of conventional doctor's dilemmas—two patients, but treatment only for one; which should be treated? The members of each pair of putative patients differed only in age, and the investigators found that the average passer by in Cardiff valued old children better than young children and older children better than adults, with a diminishing value put on advancing age. From this, the authors deduced that the man in the Cardiff street is agist, and they therefore suggested that perhaps it was ethical for agism to be built into the system of the National Health Service.[10 11]

There were two things wrong with the study. The first thing was that the investigators did not offer the respondents the option of tossing a coin. This is the equitable way of choosing between two people, but the average man in the street may not think of it spontaneously and, indeed, may not immediately recognise that it is equitable. The second defect of the study was the absence of a "control" question offering pairs of patients differing in skin colour, or in being English or Welsh. One may suggest that the average citizen of Cardiff, if betrayed into honesty, might have proved to be racist as well as agist. Would the authors then have suggested that we should build racism into the structure of the

National Health Service? Presumably not, but it would be sad if the only justification for not doing so would be that racism is illegal. However, if the 25% of the electorate in Britain that is aged over 65 started to vote tactically and became as credible an electoral threat as is this age group in the United States, we might find politicians deciding that agism should be as illegal as racism.

Older people are potential victims of the currently fashionable ideology of economics. Health economists constantly tell us that all one needs to know is the relative cost effectiveness of treatments offered to different people. Cost effectiveness underlies the ethics of the purveyor rather than the customer. If you are running a shop you want to see what you are getting back on your outgoings; but if you are a customer you have very different ideas. To take a gross example, there is a tendency to suppose that if a doctor saves the life of a 30 year old, the secretary of state for health has somehow got more for her money (our money, to be more precise) than if the doctor saved the life of an 80 year old because of the difference in life expectancy between a 30 year old and an 80 year old person. That is the purveyor's view. Other things being equal, the 30 year old and the 80 year old will be equally grateful for having their lives saved, so from the customers' point of view the two outcomes are equal. We have allowed ourselves to slip into the fast talk of the market place, without being quite clear whether we are customers or shopkeepers.

Ideology in the NHS

We might argue over the concept of a national ideology, but within the National Health Service there has to be an ideology that defines the rules of engagement. The patient has to have confidence in the ethical values that the doctor or the nurse will be following in their dealings with him or her. In a pluralistic, multicultural society, this ethic has to be minimalist, materialist, and humanist. Above all it has to be open in the criteria that are being used to allocate treatment resources. Patients come to their doctors expecting to be treated as individuals and that their particular code of values and wishes will be respected. They also expect that the health service they have paid their taxes for over a lifetime will be there when they want it. Within this implicit contract, it cannot be any part of a doctor's or a nurse's duty to sacrifice the wellbeing of any patient in the pursuit of a politico-

123

economic agenda or the profits of a hospital trust or fundholding general practice. If the government has not provided for enough health care to go round then there is no more equitable or open form of rationing than a good old fashioned orderly British queue.

The medical profession has been accused, with some justification, of arrogance in making decisions for which it has neither mandate nor intellectual competence. Decisions, implicit in rationing, that involve granting privileges to one fellow citizen over another are certainly no business of doctors. We must stand fast by the principle that such decisions are the responsibility of the nation's elected representatives, however earnestly such worthies may desire to abrogate them to others. The public can then express its opinion of priority setting at the next general election.

1 Keeler EH, Solomon DH, Beck JC, Mendenhall RC, Kane RL. Effect of patient age on duration of medical encounters with physicians. *Med Care* 1982;**20**:1101–8.

2 Kane RA, Kane RL. Self-care and health care: inseparable but equal for the wellbeing of the old. In: Dean K, Hickey T, Holstein BE, eds. *Self-care and health in old age*. London: Croom Helm, 1986:251–83.

3 Fentiman IS, Tirelli U, Monfardini S, Schneider M, Festen J, Cognetti F, Aapro MS. Cancer in the elderly: why so badly treated? *Lancet* 1990;**335**:1020–2.

4 Wing AJ. Why don't the British treat more patients with kidney failure? *BMJ* 1984;**287**:1157–8.

5 Winearls CG, Oliver DO, Auer J. Age and dialysis. *Lancet* 1992;**339**:432.

6 Elder AT, Shaw TRD, Turnbull CM, Starkey IR. Elderly and younger patients selected to undergo coronary angiography. *BMJ* 1991;**303**:950–3.

7 Dudley NJ, Burns E. The influence of age on policies for admission and thrombolysis in coronary care units in the United Kingdom. *Age Ageing* 1992;**21**:95–8.

8 ISIS-2 Collaborative Group. Randomised trial of intravenous streptokinase, oral aspirin, both, or neither among 17,187 cases of suspected myocardial infarction. *Lancet* 1988;**ii**: 349–60.

9 Grimley Evans J. The biology of human ageing. In: Dawson, AM, Compston, N, Besser GM, eds. *Recent advances in medicine No 18*. London: Churchill Livingstone, 1981;17–37.

10 Lewis PA, Charny M. Which of two individuals do you treat when only their ages are different and you cannot treat both? *J Med Ethics* 1989;**15**:28–32.

11 Charny M, Lewis PA. Choosing who shall be treated in the NHS. *Soc Sci Med* 1989;**28**:1331–8.

13 Priority setting in purchasing health care

GEOFFREY CARROLL

Health authorities are under increasing pressure to explain policies and agree priorities for resource allocation in an open manner. This requires a new approach to accountability and public consultation.[1] MPs are being drawn into trying to act as health brokers for their constituents more than ever. The Patient's Charter,[2] help lines, and public awareness of the possibility of extracontractual referrals all fuel demands for rapid access to care, often at high cost and in conflict with local health authorities' intentions and financial commitments. General practitioners, district nurses, consultants, and managers are rightly worried about lack of resources, rising demands for all services, and the difficulties of coping within contracts that are going to squeeze them even more this year.

Two shifts in thinking and action on priority setting are necessary (figure), as highlighted previously by Heginbotham and Ham.[3] The health service must move away from politicians setting the agenda and must move to a partnership between politicians and the public. More usable information is needed on effectiveness, including relation between costs, and on the impact of services on the quality of life. Expert debate and public debate are both required.

In Essex, over the past couple of years we have tried—with leaders of opinion; with voluntary organisations as support groups for localities or particular illnesses; with general practitioners as advocates for local people; and with the community health councils—to develop some kind of consensus about the problems facing

125

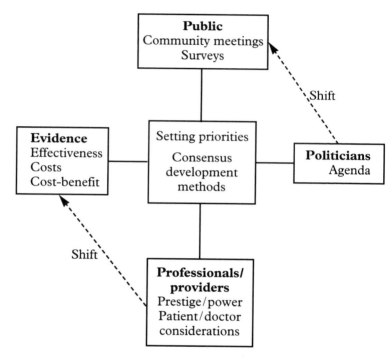

Factors influencing priority setting

us. An unpolished approach, perhaps, but one that helped, for example, to resolve the question of what to do with extra capitation funds for 1992–3. In that unusual growth situation, mental health care came out as a high priority, but with the voluntary groups wanting to put more money into community mental health services. In the end, because of the pressures on the local service and the poor physical environment, and to reduce the suicide rate of current patients, it was agreed to provide more effective acute care.

The "silent voices"—housebound people, elderly poor people— may not be represented by any lobby or action group in so called public meetings. Local consultation therefore addresses involvement of the public only in part.

Current dilemmas

Current dilemmas centre on, for example, potentially high cost patients for whom local care is absent or has failed. Protocols are

---

Box 1—Current dilemmas in health care funding

- Plastic surgery, where demand is rising for tattoo removal, laser treatment for scars or portwine stains, aesthetic changes to breasts, abdominal skin, ears, and nose
- Gender identity psychiatry and requests for sex change operations, at a cost of £5000–10 000 per patient
- Rising demand for homoeopathic medicine
- Increasing attempts by general practitioners to use the extracontractual referral mechanism to bypass long local waiting lists for joint replacements, middle ear surgery, and urological referrals for elderly people

---

necessary to define health authorities' responsibilities for alcohol detoxification and social services' commitment to residential care and rehabilitation programmes. How do the agencies cope with an increasing volume of people with alcohol and drug problems, or eating disorders, who present to their general practitioners but whose care may have to be outside the usual range of contracts because effective local care is absent? There is no guaranteed fund to pay for care for these people. How does the health authority choose who should be funded? Do we declare that funding is not available or available only within strictly limited and defined clinical criteria because budgets are fully committed? What sort of severity measures or thresholds do we use? Who should make these sorts of judgments? I do not think that as a director of public health I should be making these judgments alone and in isolation from clinicians.

Recent advice from the chief medical officer and Paddy Ross concerning the freedom of consultants to make tertiary referrals linked to guidance[4] from the NHS Management Executive challenges the contract plans of health authorities, unless the next guidance (due out shortly) defines limits to referrals. Some psychiatrists, in particular, believe they now have carte blanche to refer at will, irrespective of cost.

Other examples of current dilemmas are shown in box 1. Health authorities can address these issues more easily when resources are being increased. In a cutting climate, a plastic surgeon in Essex who believes all cosmetic surgery should be funded would find that the amount of money the health authority has available will only cover burns, emergency care, and urgent elective plastic surgery.

127

It certainly will not buy most of the other elective plastic surgery. That is genuine rationing of a regional specialty service and is a major problem, which the post-Tomlinson London Implementation Group cannot ignore in the strategic rethink of services.

Principles for resource allocation

Should health authorities publish principles for allocating health care resources? I believe, in the sense of the American Declaration of Independence, the answer is yes. The North Essex Health Authority has agreed to produce a clear statement for the public. For example: "To set health and health care priorities, allocation of resources in health or social care should be done explicitly and openly, taking careful account of values of a broad spectrum of the population in question. This must include emphasis on equity, appropriateness effectiveness, accessibility, and efficiency."

In trying to generate an open discussion about how health authorities are going to make choices about allocating resources, do some of the concepts we offer to the public—"bandwagon words" referring to equity and appropriateness—really make any sense as commitments, and can these values influence action?

Health gain criteria

Health gains have been published[5] to take account of the guiding principles deriving from Cochrane[6] and Logan *et al.*[7] They are adapted in part from similar approaches in Oregon and in Parkside and Wandsworth health authorities.

To obtain value for money, all services should be examined against the health gain criteria. In practice it will be necessary to balance judgments against these criteria related not just to proposed service developments but also to specific conditions and treatments in order to decide whether or not to provide services.

Appropriateness—To what extent does the proposal address significant health needs, identified through public comment, epidemiological evidence, or patterns of clinical practice?

Quantity—How many people are expected to benefit from the service?

Quality—What areas of health related quality of life will be most affected by the service—physical, mental, social, self care, perception of pain, sense of well being?

Effectiveness—What evidence is there that the proposal effectively promotes health or prevents ill health (that is, by improving personal wellbeing and reducing morbidity or mortality)? What is the evidence that the proposal will contribute effectively to curing or improving ill health? (Is there evidence that this service will improve people's capacity for full life, reduce pain and discomfort, or extend life?)

Empowerment—To what extent would the proposal contribute to strengthening the control local people can exercise over the conditions affecting their health and the services available to meet their health needs?

Access—To what extent would the proposal increase people's access to good quality services relevant to their health needs?

Acceptability—To what extent would the proposal improve the acceptability of the way services are delivered?

Efficiency—To what extent is the proposal an efficient means for delivering these gains?

Opportunity costs—What are the immediate and long term costs of providing the service? What other health services are competing for the resources at stake—in other words, which services will not get funds if the proposal is successful, including provider capital contributions?

Consultation on choices

In line with the Dutch[8] and Oregon[9] perspectives, empowerment of individuals and communities to influence the range of health care available requires acceptance by the people of a degree of individual responsibility for personal health care and recognition of the limits to care once choices have been determined by the community. If these principles for resource allocation are the ultimate guide then open discussion with the public is necessary to define health behaviour or needs for which individuals, rather than the state, must assume personal responsibility, and also to negotiate the limits to care. In North Essex we have tried working with a range of local people, though this is still at an early stage, mainly using proxy groups such as representatives from voluntary organisations as opposed to open public meetings in an attempt to gauge values but also to understand personal concerns, prejudices, and bias.

We have also tried with different groups to explore how to

129

represent the interests of disabled, disadvantaged, or handicapped people. Katherine Whitehorn has said that "perhaps we should not be influenced by pressure groups," but the evidence from Oregon is that groups are able to displace their own personal concerns.[10] A representative from Age Concern or Mencap can contribute to a collective understanding of what services are essential or important and what should have priority for a local community.

Other representatives have refused to participate in priority setting, preferring to insist that an increased percentage of gross national product should be spent on health care and arguing that local agreements on priorities allow the government to abdicate responsibility for improved funding of the health service.

General practitioners face a different dilemma as advocates for local people: they have to say to a patient in the surgery, "I'd like to refer you but in fact no funds are available locally for that condition." This happens already, but health authorities and general practitioner fundholders do not yet have sensible ways to help the public tolerate this, should it be necessary, until spending on the health service increases dramatically.

We used a rapid appraisal approach in a quick survey we conducted with social services and others to gain an understanding of the key health issues that concern one rural community—Maldon, near Chelmsford. We carried out interviews with selected members of the community: professionals (general practitioners, police, social workers, teachers); voluntary organisations (leaders from play groups, youth work, and clubs for elderly people); and key informants (postmen, hairdressers, local shopkeepers).[11]

How did our results relate to the national strategy on *The Health of the Nation*?[12] The answers from Maldon about priorities and community concerns did not emerge neatly as "coronary heart disease" and "lung cancer." They came out as "I am exhausted from caring for my elderly relative who can't get any real nursing support because the district nurses are run off their feet" or "I am concerned about my teenagers smoking and taking drugs, and about my unemployed husband who is getting depressed because his employment prospects are going down month by month." Neat solutions are not necessarily forthcoming, but with lateral thinking some local health issues can be addressed at substantially low cost or no cost.

The people in Maldon did not emphasise hospital based services

Box 2—Ranking exercise in mid Essex

	Rank	
Item	Public	Directors of public health
Preventive services	1	1
Care of dying/pain relief	2	5
Care of chronic conditions	3	6
Rehabilitation	4	8
Community services	5	2
Mental health services	6	4
Long stay care	7	10
Non-emergency surgery	8	7
Prevention of AIDS	9	3
Premature babies	10	9
High tech surgery	11	11
In vitro fertilisation	12	12

and waiting lists. Rather, we were told about the whole spectrum of influences on health. The priorities identified require us to make efforts to improve community transport to extend consultant care to help elderly people, and to involve police, education, social services, voluntary organisations, and the goodwill of local people in a wide range of other preventive programmes. We have now appointed two local health commissioners for Maldon to take forward the action and solutions which are not necessarily expensive and go beyond the province of health alone.

As part of the annual public health report in 1991,[13] we included an optional survey to open a debate on values, asking members of the public to rank the importance of a dozen medical treatments (box 2). It was not a systematic random sample; two hundred people completed the form, which was also circulated to all directors of public health in the United Kingdom—with a 67% response rate, plus a lot of abuse from a minority. The numbers were small, which makes the results unreliable, but the ranking exercise raised fundamental questions, and many other groups around the country have tried this sort of approach.

Chris Heginbotham has reported on the BMA survey.[14] If these

131

sort of ranking exercises are used, it is not the case that direct action will follow the answers. It would be unwise to take the answers literally, but by following the clues the values of people in the community may be looked at further.[15] What do they expect from preventive care or community services? Why does in vitro fertilisation always come at the bottom of the list? Subfertility treatment and investigation has been well researched, and there is evidence that effectiveness is improving;[16] is in vitro fertilisation so optional that it should be sacrificed entirely?[17]

As Ralph Crawshaw, one of the founders of Oregon Health Decisions, said at the Royal Society of Medicine, we must address the issue of how to search for public values in relation to health and health care and take the evidence seriously and discuss the implications for equity with the public.[18] The values of the public are not the same as those obtained from a national survey of directors of public health. That might be expected, but needs to be worked through in order to reach a better understanding of the reasons for the different perspectives. Knowledge and briefing on costs and benefits are essential to informed judgment, as has been emphasised by Klein,[19] but lay people who give reasons for making those choices should not be dismissed as ill informed people who do not know what else to say—they should be listened to as individuals who are clear about the essential factors that influence their health and about the impact of ill health on their quality of life, and who recognise our need to demonstrate the effectiveness of services.

Health authorities have a duty to participate in an informed public debate to explain and consult on key decisions. The work we have done in the Public Health Forum in Essex has encouraged managers to say in public, "This is what I have to do, these are the gaps in the services; this is what I would like to do to improve the service. This is what the change would cost; here is the opportunity cost; if I provide an extended breast cancer service, then something else goes by the board." It is difficult to compare apples and oranges, but health authorities are obliged to look at acute care, community services, and mental health services and make relative judgments about them.

Clinical priorities

It is too facile, however, to say "Let's hear from the public and then decide what we'll do." It is necessary also to look at a whole

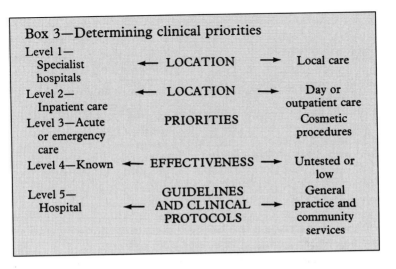

Box 3—Determining clinical priorities

Level 1— Specialist hospitals	← LOCATION →	Local care
Level 2— Inpatient care	← LOCATION →	Day or outpatient care
Level 3—Acute or emergency care	PRIORITIES	Cosmetic procedures
Level 4—Known	← EFFECTIVENESS →	Untested or low
Level 5— Hospital	← GUIDELINES AND CLINICAL → PROTOCOLS	General practice and community services

range of critical approaches to priority setting involving local clinicans and general practitioners as well as hospital doctors.

Box 3 illustrates five levels required to determine clinical priorities. It attempts to show, at the first level, our need to decide the best location of care; should it always be London, or should more work be moved to Essex and the other shire counties? Then, what is the best location of care in the sense of inpatient, day care, or general practice? There is a great deal of popular gossip about transferring money out of hospitals, which is not easy to achieve without some damage to beleaguered hospitals and which should not be done unless it has proved effective. There are for every specialty and service many unanswered and untested questions about effectiveness. There is room for experimentation and evaluation through applied research and development, rather than just jumping in feet first to stop or start a service.

Priority setting is not therefore a simple issue of what cannot be done, of "taking out all the cosmetic stuff." A whole set of questions, taken in combination, help us to reorientate ourselves, forcing us to look at the health service with fresh eyes.

On the need for guidelines and protocols,[20][21] some people say this approach should be resisted: "They are not helpful, forcing clinicians to behave in a way they do not want." Resistance will diminish, but in construction of guidelines it does help to involve

133

Box 4—Dimensions of rationing	
Choices between services	Allocation of resources to sectors or client groups
Choices within services	Allocation of resources to specific forms of treatment Allocation of access to treatment between different patients Allocation of money or procedures to individuals

the public as well, and this has been done in Wandsworth and by the South East London Commissioning Authority.[22]

Hoffenberg makes clear distinctions between the responsibility of health authorities and clinicians,[23] and box 4 shows this in diagrammatic form to convey the interdependence of these responsibilities. The upper level indicates the choice between acute care and community services (horizontal equity). The vertical line represents the choices within, say, the mental health services, caring for elderly and mentally infirm people versus children and adolescents requiring psychiatric care (vertical equity). There are difficult problems: how do we allocate the resources, and how do we choose? The lower levels within services are apparently the domain of the clinicians. But health authorities cannot wash their hands, maintaining that "it's up to the clinicians: we've given them X for renal care, now they must cope." We have a collective responsibility as health authorities to be held accountable for investment and probably for outcomes too. If there are limits, these must be explained—for example, to declare if we can fund only restricted access to care for end stage renal failure or neurosurgical care.

With the increasing public focus on subfertility, we should not simply write in vitro fertilisation off, as many health authorities are doing, or rely on the adherence by clinicians to very restrictive criteria? We have a moral duty to people on waiting lists, and they cannot simply be excluded, as was done previously in relation to surgery for varicose veins. Equally, with a rising divorce rate and remarriage common, the public has questionable expectations in terms of reversal of sterilisation. A debate is necessary to determine to what extent NHS funded interventions for what some regard as non-essential social care for healthy people are rights or should be part of a basic health care package.[24]

I make no apology for referring again to the Oregon Health Services Commission category framework (box 5).[25] I use this every day to puzzle out funding dilemmas. The framework helps in terms of extracontractual referrals; in trying to understand the context of some of the requests from general practitioners or psychiatrists or others about mental health care; in trying to help them make the decision. A common language is necessary. Are we talking about a life threatening illness, for example, somebody with an eating disorder who has a very low weight and who needs clinical care in a private facility costing £15 000 or more? Is the proposed referral for an acute, self limiting condition, and how might intervention improve the quality of life? These are blunt issues to do with resource allocation on a day by day basis. To assist decision making, some kind of framework or hierarchy of clinical need is required. If we do not like this one from Oregon which has been adapted in Wandsworth and elswehere, let us improve it.

Two direct questions must be addressed: "Do we think the saving of life is the fundamental requirement—do we always fund care to help avoid death?" "Do we have a primary duty to the elderly, the mentally ill, and the disabled which should be considered a first call on the resources?"[26] Consider those people who have chronic disease, in which treatment or rehabilitation might improve the quality of their lives.

In the health service we have a dichotomy focusing much more on hospital and related services, which have a magnetic attraction for funds. But equally a vast amount of care needs to be provided in the community,[27] not just preventive care, but simply keeping elderly and disabled people going. These questions and these choices are all reflected in that Oregon framework. Let us test the categorisation against current clinical examples and produce a better one if we think that it is flawed. But we need some way to try to place into a constructive framework these difficult ethical and clinical dilemmas about real people. Such a framework is not an ideology but an aid to decision making.

Box 5—Health Services Commission priorities by categories

Disease oriented	Rank	Health oriented
Fatal conditions		
Treatment prevents death		
Full recovery............1		
	2 ....Maternity care	
Residual problems.......3		
	4 .... Preventive care for children	
Treatment extends life and quality of life 5		
	6 .... Reproductive services	
Comfort care 7		
	8 .... Preventive dental care	
	9 ....Adult preventive care (I)	
Non-fatal conditions		
Acute condition:		
Treatment provides full cure......................10		
Chronic condition:		
Single treatment improves quality of life..11		
Acute condition:		
Treatment achieves partial recovery 12		
Chronic condition:		
Repeated treatments improve quality of life 13		
Acute, self limiting condition:		
Treatment speeds recovery 14		
	15.................... Infertility	
	16............Adult preventive care (II)	
Fatal or nonfatal conditions:		
Treatments provide minimal or no improvement in length or quality of life.............17		

Conclusions

In summary, I have set out some questions.

(1) Are all services necessary—what exclusions are possible or acceptable?[28]

(2) What are the relative priorities? Decisions must involve politicians, health authorities, general practitioners, consultants, the public, voluntary organisations, and social services.

(3) What should be the level of involvement and participation of the public through a wide range of methods?

(4) Can we agree principles for health care resource allocation using values and health gain criteria?

(5) How do we re-examine and distinguish responsibilities for health authorities and clinicians?

This approach is not just pseudodemocracy or populism; involvement of the public in an open debate on health service funding and priorities is necessary. We must have explicit principles, linked to a national health strategy and a declaration of rights to health care.

1 Carroll G. Priority setting in purchasing. *Br J Hos Med*, 1993; 49: 200–2.

2 Department of Health. *The patient's charter*. London: HMSO, 1992.

3 Heginbotham C, Ham C. *Purchasing dilemmas*. London: King's Fund Centre, 1992.

4 NHS Management Executive. *Guidance on tertiary referrals*. London: NHSME, 1992. (EL[92]97.)

5 North Essex Health Authority. *Proposal for clinical priorities*. Colchester: NEHA, 1993.

6 Cochrane A. *Effectiveness and efficiency*. London: Nuffield Provincial Hospitals Trust, 1992. (Reprint of 1971 Rock Carling Monograph.)

7 Logan RFL, Ashley JSA, Kleen RE, Robson DM. *Dynamics of medical care. The Liverpool study into use of hospital resources*. London: London School of Hygiene and Tropical Medicine, 1972. (Memoir 14.)

8 *Choices in health care: a report by the government committee on choices in health care*. Rijswijk, Netherlands: Ministry of Health, Welfare, and Cultural Affairs, 1992. (AJ Dunning, chairman.)

9 Oregon Health Services Commission. *Prioritization of health services: a report to the governor and legislature*. Salem, Oregon: State of Oregon, 1991.

10 Oregon Health Decisions. *Health care in common—report of the community meetings process*. Portland, Oregon, April 1990.

11 Gormley J, Rutt H. *Report on Maldon rapid appraisal study*. Witham: Mid Essex Health Authority, 1992.

12 Department of Health. *The health of the nation: a strategy for health in England*. London: HMSO, 1992.

13 Carroll G. *Annual public health report to Mid Essex Health Authority*. Witham: Mid Essex Health Authority. 1991.

14 Heginbotham C. *Priority setting in the health service: survey of doctors, managers and the general public on health care priority setting*. London: BMA/King's Fund, 1993.

15 Bowling A, Farquhar M, Famby J, McAllister G, Kelly R, Shiner M. *"Local voices" in purchasing health care. An exploratory exercise in public consultation in priority setting*. London: City and Hackney Health Authority Needs Assessment Unit, 1992.

16 University of Leeds. The management of subfertility. *Effective Health Care* 1992; No 3: 2–13.

17 Redmayne S, Klein R. Rationing in practice: the case of in vitro fertilisation. *BMJ* 1993; **306**: 1457–8.
18 Lansdown R. Oregon health decision, commonsense pursued. *J R Soc Med*, 1992; **85**: 501–2. (Report of speech by R Crawshaw.)
19 Klein R. Warning signals from Oregon. *BMJ* 1992; **304**: 1457–8.
20 Clinical Resource and Audit Group. *Draft clinical guidelines.* Edinburgh: Scottish Office, 1992.
21 Dukes J. *Patient protocols* Oxford: Oxford Health Care Management Institute, 1993.
22 South East London Commissioning Authority. *Specification of service for diabetes mellitus.* London: SELCA, 1993.
23 Hoffenberg R. Rationing. *BMJ* 1992; **304**: 182.
24 Borren P, Maynard A. *Searching for the holy grail in the antipodes.* York: Centre for Health Economics. University of York, 1993. (Discussion paper 103.)
25 Oregon Health Services Commission. *Report to the Governor.* Salem, Oregon: State of Oregon, 1991. (Appendix G: Ranked Categorization.)
26 Callahan D. *What kind of life.* New York: Simon and Schuster, 1990.
27 Department of Health. *Caring for people: community care in the next decade and beyond.* London: HMSO 1989. (Cm 849).
28 Hoffenberg R. *The science and cunning of physick. The Harveian oration.* London: Royal College of Physicians, 1991.

PART V: OVERCOMING THE PROBLEMS

14 Health care priority setting: a survey of doctors, managers, and the general public

CHRISTOPHER HEGINBOTHAM

The past two years has seen a great deal of interest in priority setting for health care largely as a result of the NHS reforms. The advent of the "internal market" and the splitting of purchasers and providers has raised the importance of effective, reasonable, and acceptable resource allocation.

Resources for health care will always be finite. Although this is a truism, there are obvious differences about what level of resources is required. Some believe that the amount of money available for health care should be raised substantially; others, that available resources can be used more efficiently and effectively and that ways must be found to "ration" the resources available.

The word rationing may be unhelpful. To some people the word is anathema, conjuring up their worst fears, suggesting the thin end of a wedge which will deny necessary care to more and more patients. Others have recognised that with limited resources some form of rationing has always been and will always be taken. More important, this group argues, is the way that decisions are taken, the extent to which these decisions are explicit, and the degree of involvement of the general public. Others propose that the very complexity of establishing priorities will always elude easy answers, and that what has occurred is a demand to investigate carefully the effectiveness of treatment. Only those treatments that are truly beneficial (both physically and psychologically) should be funded.

Traditionally, clinical resource allocation decisions have been left to doctors at the point of contact with patients, working within some broad but marginally elastic budget. Research and teaching have usually been linked to health care budgets in a rather loose and ill defined way so that patients can benefit from technical progress and budgets can be reallocated year on year to those areas which are expanding or increasing in cost. This rather fudged approach was possible under global budget mechanisms before the reforms, but it has been challenged by the internal market. Health authorities are now required to look much more carefully at how they allocate resources for health care.

As a consequence district health authorities, and to a lesser extent family health services authorities, must consider carefully how they allocate resources to differing client groups, conditions, and treatments. Health authorities are faced with a series of dilemmas in making these choices.

Dilemmas of resource allocation

- Prevention rather than intervention
- Saving life rather than continuing quality of life
- Primary and community health services rather than secondary or tertiary hospital care
- Individual need rather than population requirements
- Well known articulated demands rather than less popular health need

---

Much has been written during the past two years from a theoretical standpoint. Some useful practical work has been done in a number of health authorities (Southampton and South West Hampshire Health Authority, and City and Hackney Health Authority, for example).[1][2] Much of the theoretical work turns on questions of equity (equal access for equal need) and efficiency in the use of resources.

In attempting to tackle these dilemmas health authorities have discovered that available information is either sketchy or contradictory and that comparative calculations are extraordinarily difficult to make. Ethical dilemmas are posed by the use of cost-utility calculations, such as treatment cost per QALY (quality adjusted life year) generated.[3] Not only is hard data difficult to obtain but decisions made on such a basis may be open to challenge on a number of practical and theoretical levels.

Collaborative survey

Within this context the BMA, *BMJ*, Patients Association, and King's Fund agreed to collaborate on a survey of the general public, doctors (consultants and general practitioners), and general managers (in both purchaser health authorities and provider units, including trusts and directly managed units). Using a number of simple questions the survey sought to elicit the views of these groups about health care priority setting. Inevitably in such a survey many questions remain unanswered: there are no obvious right answers. But the health service reforms have placed great emphasis on the importance of "local voices" and on ascertaining the views of local people.

It is thus important to present complex ideas in ways which non-experts can grasp easily, and it is important to hear the views of the general public, even if these conflict with the views of doctors and experienced health service managers. Indeed it was instructive that several managers were critical of the simple nature of questions in the survey, notably the question (described in more detail below) asking whether the NHS should have unlimited funding or if budgets should be set. Overwhelmingly, managers—being aware of the constraints—said that budgets should be set, whereas more than half of the public would like to see unlimited funding, with the additional money being found from other budgets, such as defence.

The survey instrument

It is worth noting that the key questions within the survey instrument were developed by MORI on the basis of suggestions from the BMA and King's Fund. Although the form may appear simplistic to experienced clinical researchers, the questions were framed in such a way as to be intelligible easily to professional and lay people alike.

Each group was surveyed by a different agency with the same core questions but with a slightly different methodology. The survey of the general public was undertaken by MORI with a random sample of 2012 people, roughly equalised across geographic region, socioeconomic group, and family composition, with equal numbers of men and women. Appropriate weightings were made for small discrepancies between regions and socioeconomic status, although this seemed to have only a small effect. The MORI survey was undertaken on a face to face basis with "show cards" for the questions.

Consultants and general practitioners were surveyed by the BMA with a postal questionnaire for self completion. A return of 43% was achieved, typical of BMA surveys of this type. The core questions were the same as in the MORI poll, but slightly different information was obtained about geographical region and data. More men than women were surveyed (72% v 28%).

Senior managers within the NHS were surveyed by the King's Fund College with a similar instrument which incorporated some additional information about type of organisation, job title, and length of NHS service. Not surprisingly, a high proportion of the managers surveyed had long service within the NHS (over 10 years). Again, most were male (83% v 17%). The survey was undertaken by postal questionnaire for self completion, and a return rate of just under 60% was achieved. Allowing for the amount of job change within the health service, the return rate is probably higher than it seems in that a number of questionnaires would have been misaddressed and some respondents would have received more than one questionnaire.

Although the sample of the general public was larger than that of doctors and substantially larger than that of general managers, each of the samples was large enough to allow some general conclusions to be drawn. In total, this represents the largest sampling exercise of its type ever taken on health care rationing and resource allocation in the United Kingdom. A breakdown by social class and age of the general public sample is relevant for several of the responses. In questions 3 and 4 a geographical, social class, and age difference appeared in the response and may be significant.

Questions and answers

Question 1—Have you in the last 12 months personally been treated in a hospital either as an inpatient or outpatient, or in the accident and emergency department?

The answers are self explanatory: 36% overall replied Yes and 64% replied No. Little variance could be seen in age, social class, or income. The only main difference was that women were 20% more likely to have been treated than men, and respondents living

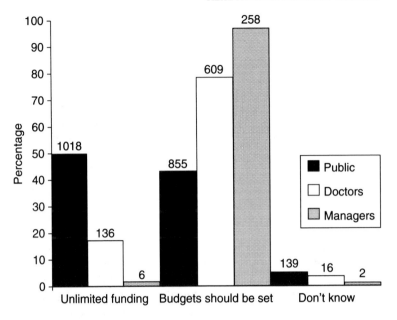

FIG 1—Responses to question 2: "Do you think the NHS should have unlimited funding or do you think that budgets should be set even if that means some treatments will have a higher priority than others?"

in Scotland and the north of England were about one third more likely to have had treatment that were those in the south east or south west.

Question 2—Do you think the NHS should have unlimited funding or do you think that budgets should be set even if that means some treatments will have a higher priority than others?

The question produced dramatically different answers from the general public and the doctors and managers (fig 1). Just over half of the general public (51%) believed that the NHS should have "unlimited" funds, but 17% of doctors and only 2% of managers had this view. In all, 97% of general managers agreed that budgets must be set, compared with 78% of doctors and 43% of the general public. What unlimited funding actually means is difficult to ascertain. We can assume (rather dangerously, it must be admitted) that no one believes money is absolutely unlimited and that unlimited funding suggests sufficient funds to meet all or most reasonable demands—but that was not the question asked, and the figures must be taken at face value.

145

TABLE I—Responses to question 3: "If additional money is needed, looking at this card, where should the extra money come from?"

	No (%) of general public (n = 1018)	No (%) of doctors (n = 136)
Higher income tax	389 (38)	56 (41)
Defence	371 (36)	59 (47)
Higher national insurance	312 (31)	49 (36)
Transport and roads	100 (10)	3 (2)
Social security benefits	79 (8)	20 (15)
State pension	13 (1)	2 (2)
Education	13 (1)	2 (2)
Housing	10 (1)	2 (2)
A combination of these sources	58 (6)	12 (9)
Other	72 (7)	17 (13)
Don't know	74 (7)	2 (2)

Perhaps the most important distinction is that managers, by and large, expressed the view that the question was simplistic and unnecessary, whereas the general public treated the question differently. This may reflect that lack of debate about the allocation of resources for health care, but certainly shows a strong wish among the general public for more money to be made available.

Question 3—You stated that funding for the NHS should not be limited. If additional money is needed, looking at this list, where should the extra money come from?

Answers to this question were analysed for the general public and for doctors but not for managers (only 2% of managers responded that unlimited funding was appropriate). Higher income tax was the most favoured option for the general public, with defence spending as a second option; for doctors is was the reverse of these (table I). To some degree this bears out other public surveys, which have shown that people are prepared to pay higher taxes (or higher national insurance, the source ranked third in this survey) to obtain better health care. The only real discrepancies between these two groups was in the extent to which they would be prepared to raid the social security budget to pay for health care. Doctors seemed to be twice as prepared to do so as the public; the public was prepared to take money from transport and roads, whereas only a tiny number of doctors would do so.

Perhaps not surprisingly, the 45–54 age range was more prepared to pay higher income tax, though there was a substantial

TABLE II—Responses to question 4: "If budgets do need to be set, who should make the decisions on which treatment takes a higher priority?"

	No (%) of general public	No (%) of doctors	No (%) of managers
Hospital consultants	1232 (61)	532 (68)	151 (57)
General practitioners	981 (49)	532 (68)	189 (71)
Managers working for local health authorities	500 (25)	Question not asked	174 (65)
General public	450 (22)	238 (30)	138 (52)
Hospital nurses	388 (19)	164 (21)	58 (22)
National managers working in Department of Health	324 (16)	177 (23)	70 (26)
Current patients	174 (9)	66 (8)	23 (9)
National politicians	120 (6)	140 (18)	96 (36)
Local politicians	114 (3)	49 (6)	29 (11)
All of above	54 (3)	141 (18)	56 (21)
Don't know	110 (5)	3 (1)	0

preparedness to do so in anybody over 25. Under 25, relatively few would be prepared to pay higher tax. Raiding the defence budget was more popular among those under 34 than in the older age ranges and diminished considerably as people became more elderly. There was a slight but not significant regional variation. Those in higher income bands were also more prepared to pay higher income tax or take money from defence, and this accords with the higher percentage of doctors who would accept cuts in defence as their first option.

Question 4—If budgets do need to be set, who should make the decisions on which treatment takes higher priority? (Respondents could indicate as many alternatives as they wished.)

Table II shows the responses to this question. The general public put its faith, firstly, in hospital consultants; secondly, in general practitioners; and, thirdly, in managers working for local health authorities. Doctors agreed that they are the most important group to make decisions, whether as hospital consultants or as general practitioners. A higher proportion of doctors than the general public stated that the public should be involved in priority setting. Managers placed a much greater emphasis on public involvement than did either doctors or the general public, possibly reflecting the substantial emphasis over the past year on public

TABLE III—Class differences in number (percentage) of general public responding to question 4: "If budgets do need to be set, who should make the decisions on which treatment takes a higher priority?

	Social class			
	AB	C1	C2	DE
Hospital consultants	244 (67)	309 (68)	336 (59)	343 (55)
General practitioners	199 (55)	248 (55)	252 (44)	283 (45)
Managers working for local health authorities	118 (32)	123 (27)	128 (23)	130 (21)
General public	69 (19)	101 (22)	135 (24)	145 (23)
Hospital nurses	79 (22)	90 (20)	96 (17)	124 (20)
National managers working in Department of Health	66 (18)	73 (16)	88 (16)	98 (16)
Current patients	33 (9)	43 (9)	51 (9)	46 (7)
National politicians	25 (7)	31 (7)	32 (6)	32 (5)
Local politicians	21 (6)	25 (5)	31 (5)	38 (6)
All of above	11 (3)	8 (2)	20 (3)	15 (2)
Don't know	12 (3)	9 (2)	37 (7)	51 (8)

involvement, especially after the publication of *Local Voices* by the NHS Management Executive in 1992.[4] Managers placed the greatest importance on the involvement of general practitioners, followed by themselves, with hospital consultants in third place.

Most strikingly, the general public would not involve national or local politicians in resource allocation decisions. Local politicians, in particular, were not favoured by the public or doctors, though a little more so by managers. The biggest discrepancy was in the involvement of national politicians. Only 6% of the general public would involve national politicians; 18% of doctors, but 30% of managers, would involve them. This perhaps reflects a concern of managers about the need for national politicians to take a greater part in these difficult decisions. Managers were also somewhat more interested in involving national managers working for the Department of Health, again possibly for similar reasons.

All groups gave a low rank to involving current patients in budget setting decisions, perhaps reflecting a broadly held view that the stress of immediate illness colours an individual's perception of what is appropriate overall policy. The general public in social classes A, B, and C1 were more likely to trust hospital consultants and general practitioners than were those in lower socioeconomic groups. On the other hand, there was very little difference in ranking between those who had recently used health services and those who had not (table III).

TABLE IV—Age differences in number (percentage) of general public responding to question 4: "If budgets do need to be set, who should make the decisions on which treatment takes a higher priority?"

	Age					
	15–24	25–34	35–44	45–54	55–64	≥65
Hospital consultants	196 (49)	218 (62)	206 (68)	196 (68)	186 (66)	230 (60)
General practitioners	180 (45)	183 (52)	154 (51)	161 (56)	134 (47)	169 (44)
Managers working for local health authorities	101 (25)	84 (24)	84 (28)	83 (29)	71 (25)	77 (20)
General public	131 (33)	91 (26)	57 (19)	56 (20)	42 (15)	72 (19)
Hospital nurses	84 (21)	79 (22)	47 (15)	59 (20)	53 (19)	67 (17)
National managers working in Department of Health	87 (22)	55 (15)	56 (19)	50 (17)	37 (13)	40 (10)
Current patients	54 (13)	32 (9)	19 (6)	18 (6)	20 (7)	30 (8)
National politicians	29 (7)	19 (5)	21 (7)	17 (6)	17 (6)	18 (5)
Local politicians	32 (8)	21 (6)	19 (6)	9 (3)	14 (5)	20 (5)
All of above	9 (2)	11 (3)	14 (5)	7 (2)	7 (2)	7 (2)
Don't know	23 (6)	20 (6)	11 (3)	14 (5)	10 (3)	32 (8)

Higher income groups would be more likely to trust NHS management, hospital consultants, and other medical staff. The view of national and local politicians was little influenced by income or age, but those in middle age were more likely to want decisions taken by hospital consultants and general practitioners than were the younger age groups, who would favour a greater involvement of the general public and current patients (table IV).

Question 5—Shown here are two types of treatment. Some treatments save people's lives but often mean they are unable to lead a normal life. Other treatments greatly improve people's ability to lead a normal life (for example, hip replacement or cataract removal) although the illness itself is not life threatening. If you had to choose between one or the other which would you prioritise? Choose one alternative only.

A higher proportion of the general public than either doctors or general managers would pay for treatment that would save lives, though by a margin of around about 2 to 1. All these groups put quality of life above saving life as a broad policy imperative. Differences may be explained by the differential response to the "don't know" alternative (table V). Most people would be

TABLE V—Responses to question 5: "If you had to choose between the two types of treatment shown here, which would you prioritise?"

Category	No (%) of general public	No (%) of doctors	No (%) of general managers
Treatment that saves people's lives but often means they are unable to lead a normal life	618 (31)	127 (16)	56 (21)
Treatment that greatly improves people's ability to lead a normal life but is not life threatening	1137 (57)	487 (62)	165 (62)
Don't know	257 (13)	147 (22)	32 (17)

expected to put saving life above quality of life, especially if it is their own life that is in danger, which makes this result particularly interesting. It seems to lend support to the policy trend for enhanced investment in primary and community health services (with a preventive emphasis) than in secondary and tertiary care, with emphasis on adding life to years as well as years to life.

The age breakdown for this question is significant. Of 15–24 year olds, 38% would put money into saving life, whereas only 20% of those over 65 would do so; 51% of 15–24 year olds would provide treatments to improve quality of life, against 66% of those over 65. There was a fairly smooth transition between these two age groups. Income seemed to have a marginal effect, with those on higher incomes likely to want life saving treatment over quality of life (table VI).

Question 6—If you were responsible for prioritising health services, how would you prioritise the things on this list?

Table VII shows the overall rankings provided by the general public, doctors, and general managers of 10 key health care areas. This result gives rise to a number of points.

Firstly, there was complete agreement about the highest ranking and the lowest. Childhood immunisation emerged as the most important priority for all groups surveyed; cancer treatment for smokers was the lowest priority. As in similar exercises (for example, purchasing dilemmas in Southampton) ranking exercises produced substantial commonality in the top 10–15% of ranked items and in the bottom 10–15%, whereas the middle group of 70–80% of items showed much greater variance, largely independent of the list length, content, and preparation.

TABLE VI—Age differences in number (percentage) of respondents to question 5: "If you had to choose between one or the other, which would you prioritise?"

	Age					
	15–24	25–34	35–44	45–54	55–64	≥65
Number of respondents:						
Unweighted base	384	423	380	296	235	318
Weighted base	398	354	304	288	284	384
Treatment that saves people's lives but often means they are unable to lead a normal life	153 (38)	128 (35)	89 (29)	96 (33)	78 (27)	79 (20)
Treatment that greatly improves people's ability to lead a normal life but is not life threatening	202 (51)	187 (53)	170 (56)	161 (56)	160 (56)	256 (55)
Don't know	43 (11)	43 (12)	44 (15)	31 (11)	45 (16)	50 (13)

Caution should be exercised in using this information, however. Childhood immunisation is almost a "given"; and cancer treatment for smokers is almost deliberately pejorative in this context, and it would be difficult to imagine many people ranking cancer treatment higher than the other items suggested. (It must be recognised that for many older people it was not known when they took up smoking that it was as dangerous as it is now known to be). Issues of "desert" are clearly apparent in these lower rankings.

Secondly, the rank ordering given by the general public was less consistent with answers to question 5 than that provided by doctors and managers. This must to some degree reflect a number of interrelated and conflicting concerns. These include

- Lack of information on the costs and availability of treatments, their efficacy and effectiveness;
- Sheer prejudice (for example, treatment for schizophrenia comes low in the general public's list, marginally above cancer treatment for smokers);
- The general effect of media campaigns and differential awareness about cost quality issues—for example, screening for breast cancer—has been widely publicised and there is now a strong gender driven debate that places great importance on screening

151

TABLE VII—Responses to question 6: "If you were responsible for prioritising health services, how would you prioritise the things on the list below, in rank order 1 to 10?"

Rank	General public	Doctors	Managers
1	Childhood immunisation	Childhood immunisation	Childhood immunisation
2	Screening for breast cancer	Care offered by GPs	Care offered by GPs; education to prevent young people smoking
3	Care offered by GPs	Support for carers of elderly people; education to prevent young people smoking	
4	Intensive care for premature babies		Support for carers of elderly people
5	Heart transplants	Hip replacement for elderly	Screening for breast cancer
6	Support for carers of elderly people	Treatment for schizophrenia	Hip replacement for elderly people
7	Hip replacement for elderly people	Screening for breast cancer	Treatment for schizophrenia
8	Education to prevent young people smoking	Intensive care for premature babies	Intensive care for premature babies
9	Treatment for schizophrenia	Heart transplant; cancer treatment for smokers	Heart transplant
10	Cancer treatment for smokers		Cancer treatment for smokers
Variance* 1.97		4.3	3.8

* Ratio of highest mean score to lowest.

for breast and cervical cancer; however, such screening programmes are expensive per life saved and thus tend to come lower in the list provided by doctors and managers;
- Genuine belief, which must be taken seriously.

It would be easy to convey a view that lack of information, prejudice and the effect of media campaigns influence the general public in such a way that their rankings should not be taken as seriously as those of doctors and managers. This would be a mistake. The public responds to information made available. If that information is insufficient then the problem of providing more information should be addressed by health authorities, managers, and clinicans. As all politicians know, the public can have a collective wisdom. The overall response given here may offer a glimpse of the preoccupations and concerns the public may have.

Answers to this question should, however, be read in conjunction with those to question 5. Many people will support quality of life measures over saving life. Childhood immunisation, screening for breast cancer, and care offered by general practitioners come high on the list, but intensive care for premature babies and heart transplants come above supporting carers and hip replacement. In other words, an emphasis on quality of life measures should not be taken to the extent of denying the availability of key lifesaving operations such as heart transplants.

There is a contradiction in these results which could be explained by a simple prejudice but is perhaps better explained by a difficulty the general public has (and this is shared by doctors and managers) in "squaring" a concern for an improved quality of life with the need to make available modern technology and lifesaving operations. Perhaps only by developing effective preventive measures will it be possible to move forward in small steps towards greater quality of life, with a reduction in need, over time, for lifesaving procedures.

People seem able to bring quite different measures to these questions. When asked what is evidently a policy question they answer appropriately—in general they would like to see more treatments that enhance quality of life. When asked about specific interventions they revert to considering how they personally would be affected. The two answers should thus be read together and a relevant compromise developed for resource allocation.

Thirdly, doctors put preventive measures and quality of life measures consistently higher than interventions. This more accurately reflects answers to question 5. The response by managers is not dissimilar, with some slight variations around the middle ranking areas (fig 2).

Fourthly, the overall variance (that is, differentiation) of the general public sample is less than half that of the doctors and managers, which suggests an uncertainty among the public and possibly a lack of key information. Perhaps the public should be involved more in setting broad criteria for decision making and the decisions then left to those able to take an expert view based on more substantial and detailed information.

Among the general public some variance could be seen in

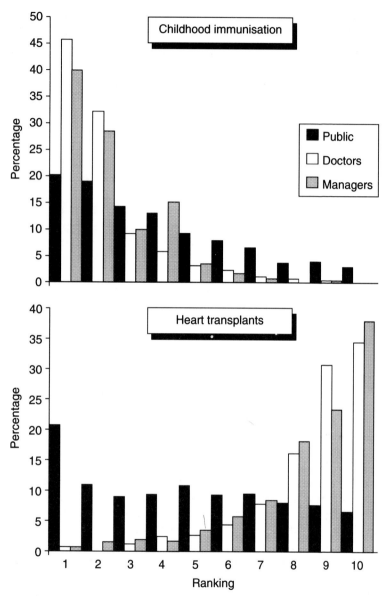

FIG 2—Ranking of a preventive measure (childhood immunisation) and an intervention (heart transplant) by general public, doctors, and managers.

TABLE VIII—Mean rankings by age of general public responding to question 6: "If you were responsible for prioritising health services, how would you prioritise the things on this card?"

	Age					
	15–24	25–34	35–44	45–54	55–64	≥65
Childhood immunisation	3.94	3.72	3.45	3.71	3.88	4.33
Screening for breast cancer	4.42	4.07	3.91	3.93	4.06	3.96
Care offered by general practitioners for everyday illness and diseases	5.20	4.63	3.93	3.61	3.51	3.55
Intensive care for premature babies	3.10	3.65	4.01	4.86	5.15	5.57
Heart transplants	3.50	4.29	5.27	5.27	4.81	5.27
Support for those caring for elderly people in the community	5.92	5.65	5.27	5.00	4.63	4.39
Hip replacement for elderly people	6.36	6.36	6.35	6.23	6.08	5.48
Education programmes to prevent children and young people starting to smoke	6.86	6.33	5.77	6.02	5.96	5.73
Treatments for patients with schizophrenia	7.07	7.15	7.62	7.41	7.10	7.14
Cancer treatment for smokers	7.44	7.87	8.08	7.67	7.82	7.58

ranking by age (table VIII). As expected, older people tended to rank support for carers of elderly people higher than did younger people, and similarly for hip replacement. Although there was some regional variation it was not significant other than in reinforcing the age difference. Those in higher income bands put greater emphasis on prevention than those in the lower income bands, as did those in social classes A and B in comparison to those in lower socioeconomic groups.

Conclusion

The results overall indicate that a great deal more work is needed to ascertain the public's awareness about healthcare priority setting and to ensure that the public is given more information about costs and benefits of different treatments. It may be that some of the difference in ranking between the public and doctors or managers is because doctors and managers have far more knowledge about the costs and benefits of different treatments.

The government should take note of the demand for "unlimited" funding of the health service. Many people would be prepared to pay higher income tax to pay for increased expenditure. More research is also needed on the public's view of quality of life as opposed to saving life, especially where this influences the criteria on which health authorities take decisions. Although the answers to questions 5 and 6 were sometimes contradictory, this should be used to develop a compromise in resource allocation; the contradiction should not simply be rejected as showing a fundamental problem. Further investment in prevention, health promotion, and "quality of life" treatments is needed, but not at the expense of lifesaving treatments. Perhaps the emphasis on effectiveness of current treatments will free up reserves for (effective) prevention and quality of life measures.

1 Heginbotham C, Ham C. *Purchasing dilemmas*. London: King's Fund, 1992.
2 Bowling A, *et al. Local voices in purchasing health care. An exploratory exercise in public consultation in priority setting*. London: King's Fund, 1993.
3 Matthews E, Meuloune E. *Philosophy and health care*. Aldershot: Avebury, 1992. (Chapters 3–5.)
4 NHS Management Executive. *Local voices*. London: NHSME, 1992.

15 Consulting the public

TOBY HARRIS

In the new, market oriented NHS no self respecting "business unit" is without its business plan. Even the NHS Management Executive has one. In most cases the list of objectives is bland and predictable, but one of those in the management executive's plan for 1993–4 is rather different.

It indicates that the management executive is to conduct a "fundamental review of health expenditure to distinguish clearly between the essential costs of high priority spending which will continue to be funded and avoidable spending which cannot be afforded."[1] This is the first time that such an exercise has been initiated in such an explicit manner at so high a level and it gives increased urgency to the current debate on rationing, particularly in the context of the current review of public spending.

The language used is, of course, carefully selected. The first point to note is that the management executive talks in terms of setting "priorities" rather than "rationing." Ministers in their public statements are equally careful. No doubt both the secretary of state and the management executive are fearful that the word rationing may conjure up grainy images of postwar austerity. In reality, of course, they are keen to avoid too many people recognising that the debate within the NHS is about people doing without particular services, rather than the oft repeated statistics about how each year more people receive more treatment.

In practice, the mealy mouthed repetition of phrases about setting priorities is not really very helpful to that debate. The issue is one of resources and is not altered by wrapping it up in words

157

that are less redolent of imagery. If there is not enough money to finance the necessary level of health services then some people will have to go without and there will be rationing.

An infinite demand?

Of course, it is argued that there always has been implicit rationing within the NHS and that this is, in practice, a feature of any health care system. This makes a number of assumptions, not the least of which is that the demand for health care is infinite or so large as never to be met. But why should this be so? Millions of people go for year after year without having any contact with the medical services. They are perfectly well and remain perfectly well—some would argue that they are more well than those who have had contact. People can have too much of anything, and that certainly includes medicines and surgery. People do not by and large seek health care for the hell of it or because, like Everest, it is there. Many people have a refreshing distrust of the medical profession and do not lightly commit themselves to its care.

Yet the view that the demand for health care is infinite persists. Of course, this is a convenient myth for secretaries of state (whatever their political persuasion) to foster. It is certainly the case that if everybody believes that the demand is infinite then everybody must accept the consequence that no matter how much is spent on health care the system will never be close to meeting all the demand. This will suit government ministers because it is then but a short step to the conclusion that concerns that not enough is being spent are a quixotic hankering after an impossible ideal and thus the government is spending enough and that everything is for the best in this the best of all possible worlds. The reality is that if we spent rather more on health care through the NHS we would find that we could go a long way towards meeting the so called excess demand, waiting lists would be shortened, and much of the current preoccupation with rationing—or priority setting as it is more genteelly called—would go away. Moreover, this would seem to be the preference of the public, at least according to the results of the BMA survey of doctors, managers, and the general public carried out by the BMA and King's Fund (p 141).

The role of government policy

The current debate is, in practice, fired by the shortage of resources which (whatever the secretary of state may say about more people being treated than ever before) is now being felt more keenly. When resources are tight the debates about priorities no longer focus on where services can be developed or improved but centre instead on what is to be dropped, restricted, or otherwise rationed.

Changes in the NHS of the past few years have also pushed rationing up the agenda. The first of these is the growth of management as a professional discipline within the NHS to the point at which it almost seems to rival in importance and influence the historical dominance of the medical profession. Managers have started to look at the cost and effectiveness of various activities and procedures in a much more systematic way than was done before. Partly this is because it is now easier to do so: more information and data are available. But imperfections and uncertainties surrounding that data call into question the validity of making what may ultimately be life and death decisions on the basis of what is currently available.

The second influence, ironically, is the Patient's Charter and its preoccupation with maximum waiting times.[2] This has focused attention on specialties and procedures with very long waiting times, which have often been those that have been deemed in some way or another as being of lower priority. One response to the charter has been to increase resources in those areas at the expense of specialties with shorter waiting times or at the expense of priority areas which need to be developed.

The imposition of maximum waiting times has also encouraged purchasers to consider withdrawing from low priority areas. As South Manchester Health Authority put it in respect of plastic surgery, "The requirement to contain waiting times for inpatient admission within specific limits, given the resource position, means that it is not possible to accept all the referrals that are received" (personal communication, 1992). Similarly, Rotherham Health Authority pointed out in relation to what they called "non-priority surgical procedures" that "the purchasing team's concern in this area arises from the Patient's Charter with its emphasis on guarantees and from the need to use limited resources in the most effective way" (personal communication, 1992).

It is hard to avoid the conclusion therefore that the Patient's Charter has had a key role in precipitating the current debate on rationing, as a result of the concentration of effort on eliminating waiting times of more than two years. The consequence of concen-

159

trating on this one indicator is that some people, instead of waiting for two years, are now waiting forever because the procedure concerned is no longer available. And at the same time some patients waiting for procedures that would previously have had waiting times substantially less than two years are now waiting a longer time for treatment previously viewed as being of higher priority.

But other government policies are also pushing the NHS towards explicit rationing. *The Health of the Nation*, for example, laid down a collection of national targets in relation to five key areas.[3] These have been incorporated in the management executive's guidance and are expected to lead to a refocusing of resources. This is linked to the emphasis on health needs assessment as part of the purchaser-provider split. The refocusing requires trying to take a comprehensive view of health care needs in an area, rather than simply making marginal adjustments to historic levels of activity in each specialty. The Welsh Office has laid particular emphasis on priority setting. Their guidance on revision of local strategies for health called for health provision to be divided into three categories: A, high priority; B, medium priority; and C, lower priority. The sting in the tail, however, was a proviso: "To help focus this effort we believe that no more than 50% (in revenue terms) of the service interventions should be classed as A and no less than 10% as C."[4] Government policy is therefore clear. Priorities must be made more explicit to enable rationing to take place.

Who rations?

The other thing that distinguishes this strategy from the past is who carries out the rationing. In the past, decisions on who did or did not get treatment were essentially made by clinicians—clinical judgment was exercised as to whether a patient would benefit from such a treatment, and people were in practice moved up and down waiting lists on the same basis. Even where the choice was one of deciding what new facilities should be created, the medical profession had a big—some would say disproportionate—influence.

Now, however, the decisions are increasingly being made by "management." Some might argue that if rationing is to take place it does not make much difference whether the decision is taken by a clinician or by a manager. Nevertheless, the process is likely to become a more open one, with all the parties involved seeking to ensure that the responsibility for the judgments made is spread as widely as possible. Government ministers will certainly try to pretend that any rationing decision that acquires adverse publicity is entirely one taken by autonomous local managers and is certainly nothing to do with the totality of resources allocated or the content of guidance issued from the NHS Management Executive.

Similarly, it can be predicted that some of the new found eagerness to consult the public is motivated by a managerial desire to have a scapegoat or at least a fig leaf to hide behind. Thus, we can expect to hear the plaintive cry as the district general manager is doorstepped by the tabloid newspapers: "Oh, but I consulted the Community Health Council"—or worse still, "Yes, but my hand picked panel of representative consumers didn't disagree with the statistical analysis I put in front of them."

Three types of rationing

Before considering this reaction further we need to distinguish three types of rationing. The first is really an extension of old style NHS planning and is expressed in the language of health needs assessment. It involves explicitly assigning high, medium, or low priorities to different services and moving resources from lower priority areas to higher priority areas. This has the effect of altering the degree of unmet need for individual services—in some cases reducing it and in others increasing it.

The second relates to the withdrawal of the NHS from a particular type of service or treatment, whether nationally, regionally, or locally. This can then be justified on the grounds that the withdrawn service does not meet health needs (because it is "cosmetic," perhaps) or that it is a proposition on cost effectiveness grounds.

The third form of rationing is rather different in that it focuses on categories of patient. For example, there is increasingly explicit debate about the case for rationing on the grounds of age. This can sometimes be justified on the grounds of cost effectiveness, but it raises serious moral issues if only because it is deemed not worth providing a particular service to someone past the age of, say, 70.

Sometimes the argument is different: should NHS resources be devoted to patients who have brought their problem on themselves? In any group of people a number will think not in relation to procedures for tattoo removal. Some begin to get distinctly uncomfortable when it is suggested that the same arguments might be applied to people who abuse drugs—or people with AIDS—or to those who smoke—or drink too much—or eat too much. The question is, if we start down this road can we turn back and, if so, what defines the turning?

This is particularly an issue with extracontractual referrals. By creating the extracontractual referral system the government was acknowledging that pure clinical freedom was effectively to be a thing of the past. Now referrals may have to go through the district health authority's sieve to receive special authorisation. Some district health authorities have protocols which mean that extra-contractual referrals are automatically rejected for certain treatments or categories of patient—this might be called microrationing to distinguish it from the other approaches we have been discussing.

How much public involvement?

If all of this is going on then to what extent should the public be involved and how far should community health councils, for example, get involved? The first thing to recognise is that the government expects community health councils to be involved in setting priorities for health services. The January 1992 document *Local Voices* specifically mentioned community health councils as one way in which health authorities should exercise their "need to listen" when assessing health need.[5] This was followed a month later by a letter from Stephen Dorrell, then parliamentary under secretary of state for health, to all health authority chairmen, in which he said, "Ministers have repeatedly stressed that health authorities should use their purchasing role to assess the relative priorities of competing claims for health service resources and to shift resources to reflect those priorities. If community health councils are to make their full contribution to the purchasing process, they must be in a position to assess competing claims and to express an opinion about the relative, as well as the absolute, value of a particular proposal."

Community health councils have always regarded it as part of their function to identify areas of pressing unmet need and to argue for the creation or further development of particular services. In that sense they have always been involved in priority setting. Inevitably, of course, lower priority services have tended to be identified only implicitly and by default.

In the early years of community health councils, one of their most important functions was to respond to proposals to close particular services. The official guidance was that the councils, like health authorities, should be prepared to make choices. Thus, the 1975 circular (now cancelled) specified that "If the community health council wishes to object to a closure or change of use, it should submit to the [health authority] a constructive and detailed counter-proposal; paying full regard to the factors, including restraints on resources, which have led the [health authority] to make the original proposal." [6]

Even though community health councils have often been involved in implicit priority setting in the past, some are reluctant to get involved in the more explicit forms of rationing, about which they are increasingly being consulted by health authorities. In particular, many members of the councils do not feel it is their role to endorse proposals to stop funding particular treatments. This can be for a variety of reasons. In some cases the view is that any system of rationing health care is abhorrent and that for the community health council to be involved in the process would seem to endorse it and undermine the council's relationship with the community it is supposed to represent. In other cases the view is that blanket rationing is inappropriate and that the cases of individual patients should each be considered on their merits by the appropriate professionals.

Some community health councils have explicitly included a caveat in any comment they might make on proposals from their health authority. As one put it: "The community health council views such decisions on priorities as being the responsibility of health service managers. The community health council would wish to ensure as far as it was able that in making priority decisions the managers paid heed to all relevant information and representations from the community health council and other relevant sources. In all circumstances this community health council would choose to advocate for all needs identified and would reserve the right to be critical of all or any of the priorities selected by the Health Authority."

But not all community health councils have followed this approach. Some have pressed for more involvement by councils

---

Community health councils involved in priority setting and rationing

Discussions and purchasers

Nottingham CHC—working with district health authority's purchasing strategy groups, focusing on policy for particular areas of work

Blackpool, Wyre, and Fylde CHC—providing a lay member to service review teams looking at particular services

Participation in priority setting exercise

Southend CHC—responded to proposed list of priorities put forward by local purchasing consortium

Four CHCs in Bristol Health Authority area—CHC members participated in a "nominal group technique" exercise to identify the key service changes viewed as being of the greatest benefit to the health of the local population

Development of participation by local people

Somerset CHC—joint research project with health authority to establish appropriate methods of public consultation

Hastings CHC—research project funded by regional health authority to find ways of involving consumers in health care planning

Bristol CHC—considering repeating "nominal group technique" exercise with representative voluntary groups and geographical forums

---

and health service users in priority setting. They think it essential that the community's values and priorities are taken into account in the formulation of decisions on priorities. Clearly, for such an input to be of any value an adequate time must be allowed for the community health council to consider the matter, and the council must be given all of the relevant information. There must also be a readiness on the part of the health authority to take into account the views it receives back from the council as a result of any such consultation.

Those community health councils that have participated in identifying health care needs and priorities as part of a local rationing exercise have been involved in varying ways and to varying extents. Three sorts of participation can be identified: discussing issues with purchasers, sometimes in specially established working groups; taking part in priority setting exercises initiated by the health authority; and helping to develop participation by local people, so that health authorities can gain some senses of community values and priorities. Some examples of these are given in the box.

Openness of decision making

Now the cynical might suggest that it serves the government's purpose if community health councils are implicated in controversial and potentially unpopular decisions. But the responsibility for a decision is not automatically shared by consulting about it. Ultimately the responsibility for rationing decisions will lie with those who take them, whether within purchasing authorities by laying down protocols for extracontractual referrals or saying that certain procedures will no longer be available, or ultimately with government for determining a level of resources within the NHS that requires the rationing decision to be made in the first place.

What is not acceptable is for these decisions to be taken secretly without the opportunity for any public debate. People have the right to know what choices are being made in their names; they have the right to express their views and the right to expect that those responsible are held properly accountable for the decisions being made. Moreover, people have those rights irrespective of whether they wish to be involved in those decisions themselves.

Community health councils can have a big role to play in this, not necessarily because they will wish to express a clear view or help those responsible to take the decision, but in ensuring that the issues involved are clearly illuminated and the implications of the choices are clear. They can act as information brokers for the wider community, empowering and enabling user groups and indeed individual patients to understand what is happening and to express their views if they wish to do so.

No doubt some will find this an uncomfortable process. Some decision makers, faced with unpalatable choices, would much rather be left alone to decide in the privacy of their boudoirs behind closed doors. However, decisions of this nature about health care are often life and death questions or, where they are not, relate to whether individuals will be able to enjoy their lives to the full. The fact that those choices are being made, and the implications, must be in the public domain.

Consulting the public will not provide easy answers, nor will it provide an easy get out when things go wrong, but it is an essential part of the democratic process. Moreover, if the public says, as it is

165

quite likely that it will, that it would like more money to be spent on the nation's health, then that is a response to which everyone, including government ministers, should listen.

1 NHS Management Executive. Business plan for 1993–4. *Health Services Journal* 1993 May 6.
2 Secretary of State for Health. *The patient's charter*. London: HMSO, 1991.
3 Secretary of State for Health. *The health of the nation: a consultative document*. London: HMSO, 1991. (Cm 1523).
4 Welsh Office. *Guidance on revision of local strategies for health*. Cardiff: Welsh Office, 1992. (WHC(92)65.)
5 NHS Management Executive. *Local voices*. London: Department of Health, 1992.
6 Department of Health and Social Security. *Community health councils*. London: Department of Health and Social Security, 1975. (HCS(15)207.)

PART VI: EDITORIALS AND LETTERS

16 On the Oregon trail: rationing health care

RUDOLF KLEIN

BMJ 1991;**302**:1–2.

The introduction of the purchaser-provider principle into the NHS will have at least one uncomfortable consequence perhaps not fully expected by its authors. It will direct public attention even more to decisions about the level and distribution of resources, both nationally and locally. In the past decisions about who should (and should not) get what medical treatment have been perceived, and accepted, as matters of clinical judgment—constrained but not shaped by national budgetary policies. In future as health authorities move towards buying packages of health care through contracts, so they will increasingly have to make explicit decisions about what they want (and do not want) to buy on behalf of their populations. Political and managerial resource rationing priorities will therefore be visible instead of being largely hidden under the cloak of professional practices. Hence the interest in the Oregon experiment, seen as the first attempt to develop an explicit system of rationing health care.[1] What lessons can be drawn for the NHS from the experience of Oregon so far?

To answer this question, it is essential to explore first what the Oregon "experiment" is about. It has been widely perceived as an attempt to put medical services in some sort of objective order of priority by using the best available scientific methods. Accordingly, it has been either hailed as a pioneering attempt to show that resource allocation can be depoliticised or criticised as showing a naive faith in scientism. In fact, the most discussed and controversial aspect of the Oregon experiment—its ranking of different forms of medical intervention in order of priority—is perhaps its least interesting aspect. The method is now being changed, and a different list of priorities will eventually emerge. The real importance of what has been happening in Oregon lies in the problems that have driven the experiment and the political processes that are shaping its progress.

Most importantly, the Oregon experiment represents an attempt to deal with a specifically American problem: rationing by exclusion. It seeks to "change the debate from who is covered to what is covered" in the words of John Kitzhaber, a doctor who, as the president of Oregon's senate, was the driving force behind the 1989 initiative.[2] In the past Oregon sought to to contain health care costs by limiting eligibility for Medicaid—the programme of last resort for the poor—and by denying even those eligible access to certain expensive forms of treatment, notably organ transplantation. The result is that only a third of Oregon's population with incomes below the federal poverty level—some 400 000 people out of a population of almost 3 million—are covered by Medicaid and that decisions about allocating funds within the Medicaid system for expensive treatments have had to be taken at public confrontations in front of television cameras. Both problems are exacerbated because Oregon has imposed on itself a balanced budget rule but has a very limited tax base, relying exclusively on local income tax for its revenue: a sense of fiscal crisis is thus endemic to the system.

The proposal for ordering medical services by priority represents the response to this crisis, as well as to the more general problems of American health care, and is an attempt to devise a financially acceptable form of universal coverage. The strategy is to define what constitutes a basic package of health care, which can then be used as the benchmark of minimum entitlements either in publicly financed programmes like Medicaid or in mandatory requirements for private insurance by employers. There are therefore powerful political incentives that make such an approach attractive in Oregon; limiting entitlements may make it possible to extend eligibility or coverage. The first step in the process is to show the nature of the trade off: to work out how far entitlements to specific forms of treatment for the existing Medicaid population would have to be cut to create the resources to cover those who now have no insurance. This is, of course, the reason for the whole exercise in ranking priorities: to see where the axe would fall. If that were all there were to the Oregon experiment it would simply mean redistributing resources among the poor; it would be a rather shabby expedient. But the expectation of its sponsors is that the exercise will produce such unacceptable results—in the sense of disclosing the denial of treatment—that the Oregon legislature will come up with more money; that what started primarily as an exercise in rationing will unlock extra resources and become a national model for expanding access to health care.

But if that is to happen Oregon would first have to show that it is indeed possible to define a universally acceptable minimum benefit package. So the argument returns to the priority making exercise— basically a fairly mechanical ranking exercise which took some 2000 conditions and calculated the cost-benefit ratio for each of them. The formula for calculating the benefits was a variant on the quality adjusted life years (QALY) approach—that is, duration of beneficial outcomes weighted by the quality of life (with the values for the weighting exercise being derived from a telephone survey of local citizens). The result produced some bizarre results—for example, cosmetic breast surgery was ranked higher than treatment for an open thigh fracture—and sent the commission charged with carrying out the exercise back to the drawing board. The commission's revised strategy is to make its approach technically more sophisticated—for instance, by seeking better information about outcomes—and also to add new dimensions. In particular, it is trying to use the results of public consultations to generate social priorities for general categories of medical intervention rather than for individual conditions: to elicit the weighting given by citizens to preventive rather than curative treatment, for example.

It will be some months before the commission produces its results, and some time after that before Oregon decides what to do about the commission's recommendations. Even the more complex, multidimensional approach now being pursued has its difficulties. Outcome measurement is not the cure all that is sometimes assumed.[3] QALY type calculations are notoriously sensitive even to minor changes in the assumptions fed into them,[4] quite apart from being open to the wider objection that they deal with the mythical average patient and do not allow for heterogeneity within conditions. Consultation exercises also raise the question of just how representative the public consulted is. In Oregon only 600 citizens turned up at meetings called to discuss priorities, and of these, 56% worked in the health care system.[5]

In short, producing a list of priorities—or defining an adequate minimum package of health care—will inevitably entail a process

171

of argument, persuasion, and consensus building. If the Oregon experiment so far has shown anything it is that there is no technological fix: imputing values to statistics and decisions about what methods to use for cranking out rankings from computers are themselves a matter for political dialogue. Technical exercises may be a useful way of starting up the dialogue and providing statistical scaffolding that may subsequently be dismantled, but they cannot resolve conflicts of values or interests.

Assuming that this conclusion is sustained by what happens in Oregon over the next year, the implications for Britain's NHS are sobering. For while technologies are transferable, political systems are not. If the Oregon experiment were all about developing a new method for determining priorities, NHS health authorities could no doubt import it fairly easily. But since the Oregon experiment is anchored in the state's political system, and relates to the special problems of health care in America, it is difficult to see what NHS purchasers can learn directly from its success or failure. Only one message seems clear. Any attempt to determine explicit priorities of resource allocation—to specific groups or services—will necessitate opening a dialogue if it is to be seen as more than the imposition of arbitrary technocratic or managerial values. In turn this implies that health authorities will have to start thinking seriously about the nature of their constituencies and how they can best generate support, professional and public, for their priorities. This means not only a willingness to argue in public but also developing a system in which they have partners in dialogue: something that is conspicuously lacking at present.

1 McBride G. Rationing health care in Oregon. *BMJ* 1990;**301**:355–6.
2 Kitzhaber J. *The Oregon Basic Health Services Act.* Salem, Oregon: State Capitol, 1989. (Mimeograph.)
3 Epstein AM. The outcome movement—will it get us where we want to go? *N Engl J Med* 1990;**323**:266–9.
4 Gafni A, Zylak CJ. *Ionic vs non-ionic contrast media: a burden or a bargain?* Hamilton, Ontario: Centre for Health Economics, McMaster University, 1990. (Working paper No 90–8.)
5 Crawshaw R, Garland M, Hines B, Anderson B. Developing principles for prudent health care allocation: the continuing Oregon experiment. *West J Med* 1990;**152**:441–6.

17 Rationing: the search for sunlight

RICHARD SMITH

BMJ 1991;**303**:1561–2.

"Every choice involves a sacrifice," said Søøren Kierkegaard. Economists recognise this truth with their concept of "opportunity cost": the cost of building a hospital is measured not merely in money but more broadly in the opportunities forgone. These might include better housing, a job creation scheme, or an anti-smoking campaign. Suddenly within health services we are becoming much more aware of having to make choices between different treatments, services, facilities, and patients. The word that has been attached to this activity is rationing—with its depressing overtones of queues and denial—but what is happening is less that people are being denied and more that the choices are becoming more explicit; in addition, broader sections of the community are taking an interest. These are healthy developments.

Doctors are less shocked by rationing than is the public. They have been at it for years. Decisions have regularly been taken not to continue treatment of terminally ill people not only because it would be kinder for the patient but also because it would be a waste of resources. Patients above a certain age have been denied admission to intensive care units; diabetic patients have been refused renal dialysis; and alcohol misusers have been turned down for liver transplants.[1] Often the rationale for these decisions has been clinical—because doctors feel happier making clinical rather than ethical decisions. But by converting ethical decisions into clinical ones they are deluding themselves, a process in which managers and politicians are happy to collude: taking such decisions in full public view is acutely uncomfortable.

Although most doctors recognise the inevitability of rationing, many people still believe that another chunk of the gross national product would solve the problem. The macrostatistics of Sir Bryan Thwaites and others showing the widening gap between what could be done and what can be afforded is one way to refute this optimistic notion,[2] but a better way may be to consider particular problems. We know that rates of coronary artery bypass surgery are lower in Britain than in many other developed countries, but this is only the tip of an iceberg of unmet need. John Hampton, professor of cardiology in Nottingham, gives a powerful lecture in which he illustrates how many patients with angina never consult a doctor; many are not treated when they do; many are never referred for exercise testing or angiography; and many don't make it to a bypass operation even when their symptoms would be much improved if they did. Professor Hampton ends his lecture with a picture of a dam, asking the audience to imagine what might happen if it burst. Or consider infertility treatment: Robert Winston, professor of obstetrics and gynaecology at Hammersmith Hospital, estimates that less than 3% of those who might benefit from the new techniques of assisted conception are actually receiving treatment—and most of them are paying. Rehabilitation services have always been sparse, while the biggest unmet need of all is probably among those caring for disabled people in the community. Here deprivation is the rule.

Most health authorities around the world are still busy fudging the issue of rationing and hoping (in vain) that it will go away, but some have now become brave enough to make explicit the tough choices that must be made in health care. First of the brave is the Oregon Health Services Commission.[3] Like most of the American states Oregon has insufficient funds to meet in full the health needs of those eligible for Medicaid. One response from Oregon was to decide that it would not pay for transplants, but this provoked an outcry from the media and a response from experts that transplantation is actually more cost effective than many other less dramatic interventions. Consequently Oregon started down the path of trying to rank medical interventions by combining the public's opinions with technical measures of cost and effectiveness. The first round threw up some bizarre suggestions, and the whole process has been conducted under a hail of criticism.[4]

But many have admired the courage of Oregon and its doctor-senator John Kitzhaber. Daniel Fox, a Harvard historian, has said:

"What really astonished me ... was the wide open manner in which the rationing debate is being carried out there. If one was searching for a classic exercise of American democracy, in the sunlight, it is Oregon's debate."[5] Together with Howard Leichter, a political scientist from Oregon, he adds: "the events in Oregon occurred mainly because health professionals who believed that these problems could be solved by reason, frankness, and good will occupied positions of authority. ... The people who created and are implementing the Oregon plan assume that the problems of cost and access can be solved by community discussion, by the application to policy of research based knowledge about assessing opinions and values and weighing the costs and benefits of medical intervention, and by legislative decisions that are accountable to voters. ... The leadership of health professionals is not the whole story in Oregon, but it is the major, and largely unreported, story."[5] Nowhere else has begun to tackle this issue with anything like the same degree of openness or rationality.

The key questions about rationing once its inevitability has been accepted are who should do it and how it should be done. The BMA's document *Leading for Health* asks both of these questions.[7] Traditionally, doctors have taken the lead, but at the operating table and the bedside rather than in open forums. Sir Raymond Hoffenberg stated clearly the traditional view in this year's Harveian oration: "If services are to be limited," he said, "I would rather see it done implicitly—unstated, unwritten, unacknowledged—in the curious and not inhumane way in which such matters are managed in the United Kingdom."

Sir Raymond has misread the zeitgeist. Democracy in all its messy splendour is taking over everywhere; older democracies like Britain are talking of citizen's charters; and professions are suspect. The decline of paternalism and the rightful increase in demands for accountability mean that doctors cannot take such decisions alone or simply within the profession. Nurses and other health professionals must be involved and so must managers; they at least are used to working within environments where resources are never adequate to pursue all projects. The difficult people to involve in the decisions are those who in the end matter most: politicians and the public. Politicians are scared by explicit rationing and become vulnerable if they run too far ahead of the electorate, but they must begin to draw the public into the debate. Their problem is that the public is more likely to accuse them of

175

meanness than admire them for forward thinking. But some politicans have begun to speak about the issue.[8]

Especially difficult is to involve the public in detailed decision making in the way that was achieved at least partially in Oregon. Health authorities may need to be much more accountable than they are at the moment if they are to make their difficult decisions with confidence, and authorities may need to look at devices like opinion polls if they are to find out what the public really thinks.[9]

The two disciplines that have the most to offer to the how of rationing are philosophy and economics, and both are building up considerable bodies of thought on the subject. Ideas that judgments might be made in terms of gender, age, income, economic value, or moral worthiness (as has often happened) become hard to sustain in the sandblaster of ethical argument, and the debate inevitably drifts back to some sort of utilitarianism or cost-benefit analysis.

Many people accept that it feels ethically doubtful to devote large amounts of resources to achieve small benefit (even if that benefit is something as precious as prolonging the life of a child) when much greater benefit could be achieved by spending those resources elsewhere. Yet many people who would accept this general line of argument become upset by the thought of using techniques like QALYs (quality adjusted life years) to help make these difficult decisions. But often the worry is misplaced: even the greatest enthusiasts for QALYs argue that they are aids to analysis, not substitutes for thought.[10] Better than abandoning them because of their many technical imperfections is struggling to improve them and to develop other techniques that will help allocate resources in a fairer and more rational way.

The debate on rationing health care in Britain has still to get fully underway in the community at large. The BMA has put it on the agenda in *Leading for Health*, but little is likely to be heard on the subject before the election. The debate should move beyond whether there is a need to make difficult decisions on allocating resources and concentrate on who should make them and how. Although it is tempting to leave the decisions to be fudged by kindly professionals, I believe that we should follow the Oregonians into the sunlight. Ways need to be found of combining public opinion with improved technical measures of cost and effectiveness to make the difficult choices inherent in allocating resources.

176

1 Moss AH, Siegler M. Should alcoholics compete equally for liver transplantation? *JAMA* 1991; **265**:1295–8.
2 Thwaites B. *The NHS: the end of the rainbow.* Southampton: Institute for Healthy Policy Studies, 1987.
3 Oregon Health Services Commission. *Prioritisation of health services.* Portland: Oregon Health Services Commission, 1991.
4 Klein R. On the Oregon trail: rationing health care. *BMJ* 1991;**302**:1–2.
5 Fox DM, Leichter HM. Rationing care in Oregon: the new accountability. *Health Affairs* 1991;Summer:7–27.
6 Mathews L. Health reforms in New Zealand. *BMJ* 1991;**303**:327.
7 BMA. *Leading for health: a BMA agenda for health.* London: BMA, 1991.
8 Beecham L. Liberal Democrats' pillars for health. *BMJ* 1991;**303**:1554.
9 Lewis PA, Charny M. Which of two individuals do you treat when only their ages are different and you can't treat both? *J Med Ethics* 1989;**15**:28–32.
10 Williams A. Is the QALY a technical solution to a political problem? Of course not. *Int J Health Serv* 1991;**21**:365–9.

18 Warning signals from Oregon

RUDOLF KLEIN

BMJ 1992;**309**:1457–8.

The Oregon experiment has become part of the folklore of the NHS. If we want to see what the future holds for the NHS, it is argued, we need only look at what is happening in Oregon now.[1][2] The role of the purchasers in the new style NHS means that they will have to decide what services to buy—or not to buy—on behalf of their populations. The implicit rationing that characterised the NHS in the past has to be made explicit: the responsibility for allocating scarce resources, previously largely diffused among clinicians, is now concentrated in the purchasing authorities. In turn, therefore, these have to choose between competing claims on resources and devise criteria that can be publicly justified. And if this is the shape of things to come where better to look for a model than Oregon—for Oregon has been engaged in precisely such an endeavour for the past three years.

In effect, Oregon has provided a laboratory in which techniques for devising rationing formulas have been tried out. The results of the experiment are therefore of great interest. Unfortunately, they are also ambiguous and difficult to interpret. So much is clear from a report of a symposium on the Oregon plan, organised and published by the Brookings Institution, which brings together the views of both the proponents and the critics of the initiative, medical and lay.[3] This suggests that Oregon holds out a warning rather than offering a model for import into Britain: a warning that there are no ready made techniques for determining choices among competing priorities in health care.

In its origins the Oregon plan was an attempt to devise an

appropriate package of health care for those covered by the state's Medicaid scheme, the safety net programme for the poor. There was a double aim in this. Firstly, the intention was to force the state's legislature to choose what health care it was prepared to finance by providing it with a ranked and costed list of procedures. Secondly, the hope was that this package would then be used as the benchmark model for designing an insurance scheme to cover the state's entire population: that it would define the basic minimum of health care protection to which everyone was entitled.

The procedures for determining the basic minimum set were both elaborate and sophisticated. They involved collecting data about outcomes from expert panels, devising quality of wellbeing scores for specific outcomes on the basis of telephone interviews with the public, and holding community meetings to elicit the value attached to broad categories of services. Nevertheless, the first ranking list produced by the Oregon Health Service Commission, more than half of whose members were health professionals, provoked much criticism and sent the commissioners back to the drawing board. The second list, ranking 709 items, was published in 1991. The Oregon legislature has since agreed to fund the first 587 items and to extend coverage to the poor excluded from the Medicaid scheme. Implementation of the Oregon plan still awaits approval from Washington.

Much of the debate in the report of the Brookings symposium is, inevitably, concerned with specific American concerns. In particular, there is much argument about the ethics of devising a rationing system specifically for the poor. However, the analysis of the way in which the priorities were determined—the mechanics of making rationing decisions—have implications for Britain. Here the differences between the first and second ranking lists are central. The first list was, essentially, a crude exercise in number crunching: the ranking of the different procedures followed automatically from the relative costs of producing given quality of wellbeing outcomes. In contrast, the second list was the product of a more complex process. The attempt to use cost-benefit or cost-effectiveness criteria was, in effect, abandoned because of lack of adequate data. Instead, the commissioners put more emphasis on community values and their own judgments about what was reasonable.

The second exercise produced a very different and more acceptable list. But the price paid for doing so, as many of the contributors to the Brookings symposium point out, was heavy. The decision making process was opaque. It is not clear what weight the commissioners gave to their own intuitions as distinct from the evidence about outcomes and benefits or community values. What started as an exercise in participatory democracy seems to have ended up, in the absence of popular interest, as a debate among experts.[4] There were other oddities about the exercise. As Robert Veitch, director of the Kennedy School of Ethics at Georgetown University, argues, moral judgments seem to have crept into the rankings: thus liver transplantation for alcoholic cirrhosis was ranked 690 whereas liver transplantation for cirrhosis not involving alcohol was ranked 366, even though the outcome for the first is as good or even better.

The problems do not stop there. Most fundamentally, the Oregon exercise conflates the various dimensions of rationing. It focuses exclusively on specific conditions and procedures. Thus it ignores, on the one hand, rationing in the process of intervention—that is, as Veitch once again points out, deciding that appendicitis should be treated is easy, but laying down what resources should be used during treatment (the numbers of tests, nurses, operating room staff, and so on) is difficult. In other words, the most important rationing decision in terms of resources may be not what to treat but how to treat—the investment in avoiding risk. On the other hand, the Oregon approach ignores the sheer heterogeneity of patients: within any broad category there will be some patients who will benefit greatly from treatment while others will not. So excluding any particular form of intervention on the grounds that outcomes are generally poor may also exclude individual patients with a good prognosis.

The main conclusion to be drawn from the Oregon experience is therefore that the notion of rationing needs to be disentangled. There are at least four different dimensions to rationing. Firstly, there are decisions about the allocation of resources to broad sectors or client groups. Secondly, there are decisions about the allocation of resources to specific forms of treatment (particularly those which require investment in new facilities) within those broad sectors or groups. Thirdly, there are decisions about how to prioritise access to treatment between different patients. Fourthly, there are decisions about how much to invest in individual patients—by way of diagnostic procedures and so on—once access has been achieved. The first two dimensions are clearly the responsibility of purchasers; the second two are the responsibility, primarily, of doctors.[5]

In none of these four dimensions of rationing is there a simple technical fix that will give the required answers. If the Oregon experiment has shown anything it is that there is no such formula, be it an appeal to cost effectiveness analysis or an appeal to public opinion. In all of them, however, there is a need to engage in dialogue about how to devise the criteria for decision making. And the means chosen to promote such a dialogue, as well as the participants involved, are likely to be very different in each of the various dimensions of rationing.

1 Klein R. On the Oregon trail: rationing health care. *BMJ* 1991;**302**:1–2.
2 Smith R. Rationing: the search for sunlight. *BMJ* 1991;**303**:1561–2.
3 Strosberg MA, Weiner JM, Baker R, Fein IA (eds). *Rationing America's medical care: the Oregon plan and beyond*. Washington, DC: The Brookings Institution, 1992.
4 Fox DM, Leichter HM. Rationing care in Oregon: the new accountability. *Health Affairs* 1991;Summer:7–27.
5 Hoffenberg R. Rationing. *BMJ* 1992;**304**:182.

19 Getting rational over rationing

TONY DELAMOTHE

BMJ 1992;**305**:1240–1.

The week of the autumn statement on next year's government spending was a good time to hold a conference on rationing health care,[1] and last week there were two.* A surprising amount of common ground emerged despite the obvious differences (the great and the good in serried ranks at the Royal College of Physicians; political activists and pensioners' representatives in the Central Hall of the Young Women's Christian Association). The points of agreement included dissatisfaction with the term "rationing" and a recognition that current data on outcomes are inadequate to allow informed choices. Everyone wanted future rationing decisions to be explicit rather than implicit, and many people were in favour of public participation in the decision making process.

Importing the word "rationing" into the debate is regarded as unhelpful because it describes, unnecessarily emotively, an everyday activity: choices have always been made between competing demands for scarce resources and always will be. What are needed are ways of deciding how to allocate these scarce resources: in the words of Professor Alan Maynard, "to maximise health to the greatest extent at the least cost."

Unfortunately, our ignorance of what medical interventions work and what they cost prevents this. New Zealand and the

* "Rationing of Health Care in Medicine," jointly organised by the Insitute of Health Services Management and the Royal College of Physicians and supported by BUPA Hospitals. "Rationing Health Care: Careless Talk Costs Lives," organised and sponsored by Radical Statistics Health Group, Public Health Alliance, Critical Public Health, Socialist Health Association, NUPE, NALGO, and COHSE.

Netherlands[2] both want to restrict their funding to a core of treatments that work but are finding the task of identifying these difficult. Salvation is expected to come through the application of outcome measures and economic evaluations of treatment. The chief medical officer, Dr Kenneth Calman, said that the government was vigorously promoting these. He listed the outcomes clearing house, the *Effective Health Care* bulletins, health technology assessment by the NHS research and development programme, the Cochrane Centre for collecting and disseminating the results of randomised clinical trials, medical audit, and the clinical outcomes group to be jointly chaired by him and the chief nursing officer.

To date, doctors have taken most decisions about limiting services to certain patient groups, particularly elderly people— whose access to renal dialysis and coronary care units has been restricted by age limits. Often what have looked like "clinical" decisions have been no such thing.[3] Few people at either meeting wanted this "implicit rationing" to continue. Decisions about which services would and would not be offered and the criteria used to make these decisions should be made explicit so that they can be debated. "Society can then debate what level of service it expects to be provided and what it can afford," said Dr W M G Tunbridge, a general physician at Newcastle General Hospital. "Doctors should not arrogate to themselves these decisions," said Professor J Grimley Evans, a geriatrician at Oxford's Radcliffe Infirmary. These are political decisions: "in a democracy they are the responsibility of the elected representatives," he said.

Involving the public in decision making has its problems. In the most famous experiment, in Oregon, they tried very hard to incorporate "community values" in ranking conditions according to their call on public finances. But the people who attended the public meetings and took part in the telephone surveys were probably not representative of those whose medical cover was going to be affected by the changes to Medicaid (the government's scheme for poor people). And there is the possibility of a clash between what the clinical outcomes industry comes up with and what people want. What if myringotomy for glue ear or diagnostic dilatation and curettage for women under 40 are shown to be a waste of time—but patients still want them?

Despite dire predictions for the future (particularly by health authorities that are losing money with the shift to capitation funding) not much explicit rationing is currently going on. Analysing the 1992–3 purchasing plans of 114 health authorities, Professor Rudolf Klein found that only 12 said that they would either not buy or would limit the availability of specific forms of treatment.[45] Tattoo removal headed the list of such treatments, followed by GIFT/IVF and several cosmetic operations. "These decisions represent merely symbolic gestures about the need to prioritise between different claims on resources rather than a serious attempt to address the issues," commented Professor Klein.

1993 promises to be much tighter financially than the past few years, when the NHS has received relatively generous settlements. Implementing *The Health of the Nation, Care in the Community*, and Sir Bernard Tomlinson's plans for restructuring London's health care will all further strain the NHS's straitened circumstances. "If the government was confident that resources were being used effectively then they would be more likely to give us more," said Professor Jack Howell, chairman of Southampton Health Authority and past president of the BMA. "Only when existing resources are optimally, effectively, and efficiently used will it be time for rationing [meaning curtailing services of proved benefit]," he said. Despite their allegiances to widely different notions of an ideal NHS few participants at either conference would have been prepared to argue strongly that such a point had been reached.

1 Appleby J. Chancellor is rough on NHS. *BMJ* 1992;**305**:1243.
2 Government Committee on Choices in Health Care. *Choices in health care*. Zoetermeer: Ministry of Welfare, Health, and Cultural Affairs, 1992.
3 Elder AT, Fox KAA. Thrombolytic treatment for elderly patients. *BMJ* 1992;**305**:846–7.
4 Klein R, Redmayne S. *Patterns of priorities*. Birmingham: NAHAT, 1992.
5 Beecham L. Health authorities are reluctant to ration. *BMJ* 1992;**305**:1049.

20 Local voices

ALLYSON POLLOCK

BMJ 1992;305:535–6.

To pursue its aim of making health authorities "champions of the people," the NHS Management Executive earlier this year issued guidance for purchasing authorities on gathering and using the views of local people.[1] Because of its emphasis on market research *Local Voices*[1] can be seen as the latest chapter in the history of consumerism in the health service. But it can also be seen as marking the demise of local democratic accountability in the NHS. It and other publications on ways of involving the consumer[2-5] concentrate almost entirely on the processes of consultation. There is no comment on the tensions inherent in consulting within the internal market. In particular, there has been no attempt to examine whether the intended result of health authorities' role as champions of the people—"decisions should reflect what people want, their preferences, concerns and values"—is feasible.

Local Voices sets out a district communications strategy based on the "imperatives" of listening, informing, discussing, and reporting. It also includes a list of well established market research techniques, ranging from patient satisfaction questionnaires to interviews, complaints procedures, and public meetings, with 19 examples of good practice.[1] There are, however, many difficulties with the listen, discuss, inform, and report approach.

First is the issue of representation. Purchasers struggle to understand whose views are being listened to. Since community participants are usually identified by community health councils it is sometimes unclear whether they are representing individuals, groups within the community, or the voluntary sector, and this becomes especially important when changes in service provision or priorities are proposed.

Secondly, discussions among purchasers, providers, and community participants often show a mismatch between professional and lay perceptions of need. For example, consumer representatives often complain about the dominance of the medical model in mental health and other services. Such conflicts are not easily resolved when resources are insufficient to cope with current workloads, let alone to develop new innovative services. Moreover, discussions which expose "unmet need" may result in community participants being asked to identify what elements of current service provision should be forgone. Again this raises the question of the legitimacy of local decision making in the absence of democratic structures for local accountability.

Thirdly, despite anguished debates about priorities and rationing there is no discussion on why the government is abdicating responsibility for resource allocation by devolving decisions to local managers and individual members of the public. Formerly health care judgments were depoliticised through clinical decision making, where at least there was some technical expertise to inform a complex debate.

Fourthly, attempts by purchasers to inform discussions and debates are hindered by the absence of information on outcomes, costs, and effectiveness. Many purchasers and providers are still unfamiliar with the type and range of information required to evaluate quality and outcome of services. Complex technical issues are not always easily shared even with people working within the service.

Finally, how do purchasers report back to community participants when they are faced with having to admit that there are insufficient data and resources to develop suggested innovations in services, and how do purchasers explain the complex symbiotic relations between purchasers and providers without committing political suicide?

Consumerism in the NHS is not new, and was partly responsible for giving rise to community health councils in 1974.[7] However, criticism of community health councils' lack of representativeness and power, and the ambiguity of their role as observers at health authority meetings,[8][9] resulted in the green paper *Patients First* proposing their abolition in 1979.[10] But in the days when a government would publish the responses to consultation, and the secretary of state could write in its foreword, "It is important for the public . . . to judge how far these decisions have been supported or opposed," the consultation disclosed much public support for community health councils.[11]

Local Voices now implies that the long stay of execution may be over. As health authorities seek direct access to groups and individuals in the community the role of the community health council diminishes. But by reducing public participation to individual consultation, reasoned responses and protests by the public to changes in the NHS are also made harder.

Local Voices does not mention the consultation process which existed up until 1991. Although local democracy was considerably weakened in the second NHS reorganisation in 1982, district health authorities still included local authority representatives. The white paper's justification for reconstituting health authorities with all five non-executive members nominated by the regional health authority was that "the [former] DHA was neither truly representative (of the local community) nor a management body." Hence "authorities based upon this confusion of roles would not be equipped to handle the complex managerial and contractual issues that the new system of matching resources to performance will demand."[12] It remains to be seen whether the expansion of the new management role of DHAs to include being champions of the people will restore this confusion of roles.

Members report that health authority meetings since the 1991 changes have been more comfortable and friendly and that decision making is easier,[13] especially since they are increasingly held in private.[14] But there has been little debate on the impact of membership on the new reforms or on the effect of large purchasing consortia and district mergers, which remove health authority members still further from their communities.[14]

The model of direct ministerial management of health care, with its focus on individual consultation, is a long way from the 1944 green paper, which originally intended that local authorities should run health services and special professional and technical guidance would be provided by local health services councils.[15] Then, in rejecting the suggestion that experts should be included in local authority administration of health services, the government felt, "The risk of impairing the principle of public responsibility (accountability)—that effective decisions on policy must lie entirely with elected representatives answerable to the people for the decisions that they take—outweighs any advantages likely to accrue."

Recent research shows that local democracy does count.[16 17] Regardless of their political opinions, people identify with and value the role of their local authorities in decision making. Many of the debates throughout the 1980s indicate that there is no reason to believe that they would not support a more democratic health service.[18 19]

If the NHS Management Executive is having second thoughts about whether the new district health authorities and their members can fulfil their management role and be champions of the people then it has to realise that market research models can never be a substitute for a democratic process and local accountability. Otherwise community consultation, consumerism, and participation in needs assessment, priority setting, and developing and monitoring service specifications are meaningless.

1 NHS Management Executive. *Local voices. The views of local people in purchasing for health*. London: NHSME, 1992.
2 National Consumer Council. *Involving the community. Guidelines for health service managers*. London: NCC, 1992.
3 Winn L, ed. *Power to the people. The key to responsive services in health and social care*. London: King's Fund Centre, 1990.
4 McIvor S. *Obtaining the views of health service users*. London: King's Fund Centre, 1991.
5 Levenson R. Joule N. *Listening to people. User involvement in the NHS—the challenge for the future*. London: Greater London Association of Community Health Councils, 1992.
7 Farrel C, Levitt R. *Consumers, community health councils and the NHS*. London: King's Fund Centre, 1980.
8 Royal Commission on the NHS. *Report*. London: HMSO, 1979.
9 Hogg C. *The public and the NHS*. Birmingham: Association of Community Health Councils in England and Wales, 1986.
10 Department of Health and Social Security. *Patients first: consultative paper on the structure and management of the NHS in England and Wales*. London: HMSO, 1979.
11 Department of Health and Social Security. *Patients first: summary of the comments received on the consultation paper*. London: DHSS, 1990.
12 Department of Health. *Working for patients*. London: HMSO, 1989.
13 Ashburner L, Cairncross A. *Authorities in the NHS. Members: attitudes and expectations*. Warwick: University of Warwick Centre for Corporate Strategy, 1992. (Research for Action, Paper 5.)
14 Ham C, Matthews T. *Purchasing with authority: the new role of DHAs*. London: King's Fund College, 1991.
15 Ministry of Health, Department of Health for Scotland. *A National Health Service*. London: HMSO, 1944.
16 Broom D. Does local democracy count? *Search* 1991;Nov 11:5–7.
17 *Attitudes to local government. A survey of electors*. York: Joseph Rowntree Foundation, 1991.
18 *Community-consumer representation in the NHS, with specific reference to community health councils*. London: Greater London Association of Community Health Councils, 1989.
19 Greater London Council. *Accountability and democracy in London's health service*. London: GLC, 1986.

21 "Mind the gap": reflections of an American health maintenance organisation doctor on the new NHS

JAMES E SABIN

BMJ 1992;**305**:514–6.

As I prepared to return to the United States after a three month sabbatical to study ethical dimensions of the NHS changes since *Working for Patients*, an unlikely phrase from the London Underground kept presenting itself—"Mind the gap!"

I eventually discerned four "gaps" that capture the lessons I would take back to the United States and the suggestions I wanted to leave in the United Kingdom. Firstly, a gap between the health care you want and the money you are willing to spend. Secondly, a gap in communication between doctors and patients about the economics of the NHS. Thirdly, a gap between two cultures—described by the new secretary of state for health, Virginia Bottomley, as "the world(s) of medicine and management."[1] Finally, a gap in medical ethics between old precepts and new circumstances. If you address these gaps effectively the NHS will be a model for the twenty first century. If you do not you will undermine what many of my interviewees called a "national treasure."

Gap between you want and what you will pay for

Even though the United States spends 270% more per capita than the United Kingdom on health care, American doctors, like

189

their British counterparts, complain about underfunding. What distinguishes the two countries is not the perception of a funding gap, but the profoundly different values each uses to determine how much to spend in the first place. Where the United States is driven by the rights of individuals, the United Kingdom has emphasised the needs of communities.

During my visit I encountered tremendous interest in the Oregon experiment, but the experiment in the United Kingdom is far more radical. Oregon is preparing to purchase health care for a portion of the population in a single state. In the United Kingdom every district health authority has been purchasing health care for its entire population since 1 April 1991. I do not believe, however, that politicians or the public yet realise how revolutionary and explosive the bureaucratic-sounding "separation of purchaser from provider" is likely to be.

If I were forced to identify the most demanding ethical task in the NHS at present I would choose purchasing. I admire but do not envy the leaders of the South East London Commissioning Agency (representing the Camberwell, Lewisham and North Southwark, and West Lambeth District Health Authorities), who so boldly accept what Americans call the "hot seat":

[We will] target our resources, following an evaluation of health care needs, so as to gain the greatest improvement in our population's health ... We will aim for a comprehensive service to achieve genuine health gains, but as we have limited resources we will be explicit about those needs which can be met and those which cannot.[2]

Their intentions are breathtaking. Public officials prefer to waffle about hard choices, but there is no waffling here. The agency resoundingly endorses utilitarian values, with no mention of individual rights. Success will be measured by improved community health. The agency makes no promises to individuals. It boldly commits itself to telling the truth when it does not provide for a need, rather than doing what I have often observed in the United States—disingenuously changing terms and redefining the unmet "need" as a "preference" or "demand."

All the purchasers I talked with, however, worry that although they have statutory authority to purchase for their districts, they do not have real legitimacy in the eyes of the district population, which is barely aware of the whole idea of purchasing. As I work at a health maintenance organisation I find that comparing district health authorities with health maintenance organisations helps to clarify the issue of legitimacy. Like district health authorities, health maintenance organisations provide all the care for 15% of the American population on a prepaid basis. Unlike district health authorities, members of health maintenance organisations are not automatically "enrolled" according to where they live—they decide each year whether to belong to them. Their enrolment confers legitimacy on the organisation. A dissatisfied member can "fire" the health maintenance organisation and join another programme. On average 5–10% of members do this each year.

District health authority purchasers are trying to cultivate legitimacy by doing surveys, creating forms of dialogue with their communities, and deepening their ties with general practitioners, but their position is highly vulnerable. At the same time that the South East London Commissioning Agency defines its mission as purchasing for the community by utilitarian values, the patient's charter invites highly individual expectations by using American style language of rights—"every citizen has [a right] to receive health care on the basis of clinical need."[3] I fear that entities like the commission may not be able to sustain their utilitarian ethic when they find—as ultimately they must—that they cannot meet some of the real needs of real people, and shrouds begin to wave.

The highly exposed position of the district health authority as purchaser leads me to make three predictions. Firstly, central government will rapidly come under tremendous funding pressure from district managers. One purchaser told me that while "parliament may have hoped that establishing districts as purchasers would build a moat between the national government and resource pressure, they are living in cloud cuckoo land if they think the changes will really insulate them." Secondly, well before the debate between implicit and explicit rationing, which was launched in this journal in January 1991, is settled the public will realise that rationing is a fact of life in the districts and you will enter a period of heated moral and political controversy.[4] Finally, although citizens effectively have no choice about their districts, which creates a severe problem of legitimacy, they can "hire and fire" their general practitioner. I predict that fundholding general practitioners will join with hospital trusts to form new entities providing primary, consultant, and hospital care, much as American health maintenance organisations do. Like district health authorities these entities will have to ration, but they will diminish the problem of legitimacy by giving the citizen a choice regarding membership, the way American health maintenance organisations do.

Communication gap between doctors and patients

A general practitioner whom I asked about his experiences discussing resource allocation with patients told me the following story.

Shortly after I began to practise a patient consulted me about a cough. She wanted an antibiotic, which wasn't clinically indicated. Instead of just saying that I would prescribe what she needed and that she didn't need an antibiotic, which is the kind of thing I usually say, I said something like— "we shouldn't waste money on an antibiotic when you don't need it so we will have resources available when you do." All she heard was the word "money." She went home all worked up, and the next thing I knew the cough had turned into pneumonia and she really did need the antibiotic!

Many doctors told me anecdotes of this kind—generally humorous. I came to regard these as "cautionary fables," designed to warn that discussing money with patients is dangerous. Others told me how disturbed and even angry they were on the relatively rare occasions when patients asked them if cost considerations had influenced their thinking. Doctors seem to feel stronger taboos against discussing money than sex.

Patients seemed much readier to acknowledge resource limitations and talk about them than their doctors were. Sitting with general practitioners in their surgeries, I noted how regularly patients moved rapidly into the office and presented a focused agenda, recognising and accepting the fact that the doctor had little time and many patients. I was able to ask patients about their behaviour, and I satisfied myself that they acted as they did from a realistic recognition of the limits on collective resources, not low self esteem or inability to ask for anything for themselves.

As a psychiatrist I was especially moved by a story told by the father of a 26 year old man with schizophrenia, which became emblematic for me of how much the British view health care as a community resource rather than an individual right.

Robin had been getting increasingly psychotic, deluded, and agitated during the previous few weeks. He has been ill for five years, since his first attack as an undergraduate at Cambridge. He had always lived with us since then, and we recognised the signs that he was going downhill fast. But our general practitioner told us there was a waiting list, and the psychiatrist said he was not ill enough yet. Over Christmas, he was driving us up the wall. He was very trying. Then on New Year's Day, he got really psychotic. I lost my temper and forced the system. I physically ejected my own son from the house and told him to go to the police. I knew they could make the hospital admit him. ... I feel terribly guilty about the whole thing, having to use coercion, putting the police and the hospital on the spot, but we were desperate. I may have been doing a more deserving patient out of a bed. One should not have to descend into this wheeling and dealing.[5]

I am convinced that users of the NHS, like Robin's father, are ready to collaborate with their doctors in seeking to manage limited resources fairly but that doctors in the United Kingdom as in the United States are just beginning to learn how to join with them. Thirty years ago doctors believed it was harmful to discuss terminal illness and told cautionary tales about patients who gave up hope or committed suicide on receiving a diagnosis of cancer. We have since learnt how to make bad news part of good care, and I anticipate that we will have to do the same with the new economic factors that impinge on medical practice.

Gap between medical and managerial cultures

For an American doctor, Rudolf Klein's analysis of the "radical transformation" that *Working for Patients* engendered in the NHS provides an experience of déjà vu. According to Klein, the 1948 "concordat" between the state and medical profession, which gave doctors a degree of autonomy and government a level of budgetary control well beyond anything we have ever had in the United States, is now undergoing fundamental change.[6] The terms Klein uses to describe the transition from an era of professional "status," when the state trusted doctors to govern themselves in accord with public interest, to a relationship of "contract," in which the medical profession becomes accountable to managers, could easily come from an American medical journal of 10 years ago.

As a foreigner I was allowed to enter rival medical and managerial camps much as the Red Cross can do in battle zones. One highly committed doctor described management as "the syphilis of the NHS." An equally committed manager said that "before the reforms the NHS was run by consultants who in the past would have been buccaneers on the high seas." Yet despite the profound distrust between medicine and management virtually every encounter also gave evidence of shared ideals.

The special representative meeting of the BMA in March of 1992 showed a profession in turmoil and some disarray. The group enthusiastically endorsed motions that affirmed utterly incompatible positions. Moments after the representatives condemned "fixed budgets" and any restriction on "freedom of choice for patients and their doctors," they agreed—by a similar majority—"that rationing of health care is inevitable." Surely rationing will require fixed budgets and restrictions of choice!

Gatherings of American doctors show similar fiery rhetoric, inconsistent positions, and volatile moods. Rapid change elicits symptoms of adolescence on both sides of the Atlantic. These growing pains are probably healthy signs of our profession struggling to adapt. I was much more alarmed by the degree of hostility within the BMA between those who believe the NHS changes must be fought without compromise and those who want to get on with the task of caring for patients and making the changes work as well as possible. A visitor can only hope that you in Britain will be more successful than we in the United States have been at distinguishing principles that should be fought for from habits and vested interests that may be painful to relinquish but do not reflect the ethical core of medicine.

Virginia Bottomley wants "the world(s) of medicine and management to coexist comfortably."[1] My observations suggest that your effort to embrace both "traditional collective responsibilities" and "the new consumerism" will create too much tension for comfort.[7] "Effective collaboration with tolerable levels of conflict" would be a more realistic objective for Mrs Bottomley. The NHS of the future will need managerial as well as medical virtues. To bridge the gap between the two cultures, however, you will need imaginative leadership from the secretary of state for health, the BMA, and the royal colleges.

Gap between traditional medical ethics and the new NHS

Doctors in both the United States and the United Kingdom are struggling to develop ethical precepts for circumstances in

194

which—to use Marshall Marinker's terms—they face the "[daunting] prospect of being at once the advocate for the individual patient and the arbiter of distributive justice for the practice population."[8] Despite the power of the taboo against discussing rationing explicitly with patients I believe that you in the United Kingdom have progressed further than we have in the United States.

Doctors in the United States still ask if it is unethical to consider cost in making treatment recommendations. The American Medical Association's code of ethics provides no guidance. The BMA code does: "It is the doctor's ethical duty to use the most economic and efficacious treatment available."[9] At the special representative meeting of the BMA delegates presented 27 separate motions affirming the need for rationing. The question for you is not whether to set priorities and ration but how to do it.

The best opportunity to develop the new ethics may be in teaching medical students and young doctors. Here are vignettes from three superb small group discussions in the general practice clerkship at Guy's and St Thomas's Hospitals. They illustrate how students and faculty can explore how to balance fiduciary attention to patients and stewardship of public resources.

The general practitioner advised a man with cellulitis to enter the hospital for intravenous antibiotic treatment, but the patient was adamant in refusing. The students debated "beneficence" (caring for his cellulitis) versus "automony" (respecting his wish to remain at home). When I described the use of home intravenous antibiotic treatment at my health maintenance organisation, the students recognised that it might be possible to treat the cellulitis (beneficence), respect the patient's wish to be at home (autonomy), while at the same time reducing the cost of the treatment (justice)—a superior clinical and ethical outcome.

The man with a cough secondary to lung cancer wanted an antibiotic which the general practitioner thought was not clinically indicated. Half of the students favoured prescribing it—largely to strengthen the doctor-patient relationship. The other half thought this would be a bad precedent and opposed prescribing the antibiotic. I noted that no one had mentioned cost and asked if it would matter whether the antibiotic cost £5 or £100. In the discussion that followed one student said,—"I guess we have to manage medicine in a businesslike way ... what we spend in one area could have helped people somewhere else."

A young couple asked the general practitioner for a chromosome test to establish the paternity of their baby. The students discussed the complex issues involved in counselling the couple and deciding how to respond to the request. When I asked them, "If you decide it is clinically the right thing to do, is it the kind of service the NHS funds should pay for?" they moved into a vigorous debate about the goals of health care and need to set priorities.

In the next several years medical schools throughout the United Kingdom, like St Bartholomew's and the London Hospital Medical School,[10] Oxford, and the United Medical and Dental Schools of Guy's and St Thomas's Hospitals, will be experimenting with new ethics curricula. At the same time the Central Ethical Committee of the BMA will be writing the next edition of *Philosophy and Practice of Medical Ethics*. My colleagues and I from the United States will be avidly watching your progress.

Conclusion

We Americans desperately need to learn how to extend good health care to our entire population and at the same time set limits on spending. Developments in the United Kingdom could teach us a great deal. Until now, however, Americans have used the notorious NHS waiting lists, and our suspicion that the United Kingdom places substantially less value on the strong forms of doctor-patient partnership and informed consent that we cherish, to discount the lessons of your impressive accomplishments.[11]

But we will not be able to avoid learning from the NHS much longer. As Rudolf Klein has shown, our two systems are converging.[12] The United States may procrastinate, but we will inevitably provide health care to all our citizens, and the recent election ensures that the NHS will continue to develop an "internal market."

The medical profession in the United Kingdom has been traumatised and is now in a zone of choice. Resisting the changes engendered by *Working for Patients* might seem to be the simpler course, but it will not succeed. For better or worse, all first world economies are currently using market mechanisms as a major form of control. The effort in the United Kingdom to blend the social values of the NHS with market structures could create a prototype for the next century. Success, however, will require developing skill at district level at involving the public in setting priorities and rationing, improving doctors' skills at collaborating with patients to manage resources, creating rapprochement between medical and managerial cultures, and adopting new ethical precepts for the new circumstances. If you are able to mind these gaps your model will be one from which other countries, especially the United States, can learn crucial lessons.

JES was a visiting fellow at the Centre of Medical Law and Ethics, King's College, University of London, from February to April 1992.

1 O'Sullivan J. Bottomley would shut uneconomic NHS hospitals. *Independent* 1992 Apr 17:7.
2 South East London Commissioning Agency. *Aiming for the best of health.* London: SELCA, 1991:4,9.
3 Department of Health. *The patient's charter.* London: HMSO, 1991.
4 Smith R. Rationing: the search for sunlight. *BMJ* 1991;**303**:1561–2.
5 O'Sullivan J. Hospital crises breaks a family. *Independent* 1992 Mar 8:9.
6 Klein R. From status to contract: the transformation of the British medical profession. In: L'Etang H, ed. *Health care provision under financial constraint: a decade of change.* London: Royal Society of Medicine, 1990:127–34.
7 Klein R. *The policies of the National Health Service.* London: Longman, 1989:197.
8 Marinker M. Changes and developments in primary care. In L'Etang H, ed. *Health care provision under financial constraint: a decade of change.* London: Royal Society of Medicine, 1990:141–8.
9 British Medical Association. *Philosophy and practice of medical ethics.* London: BMA, 1988:72.
10 Doyal L. Teaching ethics at Bart's and The London. *Bulletin of Medical Ethics* 1991; September:19–22.
11 Schwartz R, Grubb A. Why Britain can't afford informed consent. *Hasting Center Report* 1985;**15**(August):19–25.
12 Klein R. The American health care predicament: spending more, feeling worse. *BMJ* 1991;**303**:259–60.

22 Letters to the editor

18 January 1992

EDITOR,—Richard Smith's editorial on rationing (p 173) implies that I expressed paternalistic, indeed undemocratic, views in my Harveian oration.[1] I should like to try to explain myself.

Like others with whom I've debated the issue Smith fails to distinguish between rationing and determining priorities. In determining priorities, I agree, everyone should be involved— doctors, nurses, other health professionals, managers, and the general public—and I made this point in my oration. This is what happened in Oregon. As Smith says, the process was not easy and some rather bizarre proposals emerged first time round; the latest, much improved set of priorities was arrived at with the help of medical advice and guidance. This professional role is neither paternalistic nor improper: I would not feel competent to vote on the best way to provide our energy needs over the next few decades without the advice of physicists.

Rationing is something different. It is the deliberate withholding of certain services because of costs or lack of facilities or staff. It is a policy decision, one that is taken by the government or a health authority, not by the public. An example of successful rationing was the government's prohibition of heart transplantation in 1973. It was accepted because the public at the time had strong ethical reservations about the operation anyway; I suspect that it would not be accepted today. An example of unsuccessful rationing was the attempt some years ago by West Midlands Regional Health Authority to impose a limit on the number of patients admitted to a renal dialysis programme because the budget was overspent. The doctors in charge of the programme objected furiously and publicised the issue, and as a result the restriction was withdrawn. My sympathies were with the doctors: they were the ones who had to tell patient number $x + 1$ that, although he was an otherwise fit young man ideally suitable for dialysis, he would have to go home to die because they had used up their quota of x places on the programme. This sort of explicit rationing by authority forces doctors to make unpalatable, indeed unacceptable, decisions at the bedside or in the clinic. Of course, they object. Why should they function as the authority's hatchet men?

If rationing is to be explicit I believe that it will work only if a defined block of services is withdrawn or withheld, such as bone marrow transplantation or in vitro fertilisation. The public—and the doctors—then know that these services are not available; like it or not, there is no choice. In deciding which whole service to exclude a wise government or authority would take account of the public's view of priorities and delete those placed at the bottom of the public's list or face the electoral consequences.

Anything less than an absolute embargo on specific services places clinicians in an extraordinarily difficult position. Which patients should they select for their annual quota of coronary bypass operations? Should they reserve judgment on a particular patient in case a more deserving one comes along to take up the last quota place? Such decisions are being made today by individual doctors dealing with individual patients, most starkly by those with tight budgets. It is this sort of rationing that I would prefer to see implicit rather than explicit, not through a belief in medical imperialism or paternalism but through a concern about the anguish that patients and their relatives might feel if they knew that they are being denied services that other patients had received explicitly because of cost.

Smith might wish to argue—and I might be persuaded to agree—that this sort of explicitness is precisely what is needed to open people's eyes to the present government's parsimonious attitude to our NHS. In my Harveian oration I made the point that if we spent as much on our health service as the average for countries in the Organisation for Economic Cooperation and Development we could probably meet all reasonable clinical demands now and for some time to come at a level inferior to none—that is, serious rationing could be deferred almost indefinitely.

Sadly, I suspect that our NHS will remain underfunded. I strongly support Smith's plea for more public debate about medical priorities and rationing. This is what I intended my Harveian oration to stimulate.

RAYMOND HOFFENBERG

1 Smith R. Rationing: the search for sunlight. *BMJ* 1991;303:1561–2. (21–28 December.)

28 August 1993

EDITOR,—Recently there has been a progressive contraction of the resources made available for health care in New Zealand, a trend that many other countries including the United Kingdom have experienced. These financial constraints have led to increasing instances of treatment rationing or compromise. We wish to inform our British colleagues of a ruling by a New Zealand hospital ethics committee that has been lauded in the New Zealand media as a landmark decision. The Wellington Area Health Board Ethics Committee was asked two questions:

(1) Is it ethically justified in times of resource constraint to compromise the treatment of one group of patients for the benefit of another? The committee's clear advice was that such rationing of treatments (euphemistically termed prioritisation) was appropriate. However, they also advised that if it was perceived that the service was "unduly penalised in the overall structure" then the instigator of the resource constraint (management) should be approached for a review.

(2) In the situation where the optimum treatment for a patient is compromised because of fiscally directed resource constraints, is the clinician ethically required to inform the patient of this and of the possible consequences as they relate to increased side effects and reduced effectiveness of treatment? The committee answered, "The issue of informing patients comes under the principle of veracity or truth telling . . . it is important that the patient be given the truth about the parameters of treatment available . . . and the fact you would like to do more but within constraints it is not possible."

We believe that the committee's replies have important implications for all contemporary clinical practice. We suggest that the practice of clinicians concealing from the patient the consequences of treatment compromise is common and has developed because of a humanitarian concern that such information serves no thera-

200

peutic benefit and could probably increase the patient's anxiety. The Wellington Area Health Board Ethics Committee has indicated that this approach is no longer acceptable. We agree, and we feel that this approach is an example of the type of paternalism that public opinion in New Zealand has repeatedly denounced in recent times. We imagine that the same applies in the United Kingdom.

This ethical ruling is a landmark decision that instructs clinicians to be open and honest with their patients concerning issues pertaining to treatment rationing. By citing "reasons of corporate and competitive confidentiality" (the current management phrase in New Zealand) administrators may attempt to gag clinicians faced with resource constraints. The ruling of the ethics committee protects those who speak out from the offensive label of "opportune shroudwavers out for their own gain."

It is a chilling thought that clinicians believing that concealment is humanitarian are in effect colluding with the aims of administrative systems that are developing rationing covertly.

N A SPRY
D S LAMB
P J DADY

11 September 1993

EDITOR,—Chris Ham (p 59) drew attention to some of the problems of comparing different services,[1] but his analogy of comparing apples, oranges, and kiwi fruit is incomplete. The missing element is that we would be comparing an apple for *him* to an orange for *you* and a kiwi fruit for *me*. In other words, this is not merely about comparing the value of fruit. It also involves comparing the fruitworthiness of different people—a much more complex issue.

J E LEESON

1 Ham C. Priority setting on the NHS: reports from six districts. *BMJ* 1993;**307**:435–8. (14 August.)

Index